C-1

C-4

C-2

C-3

C-5

C-6

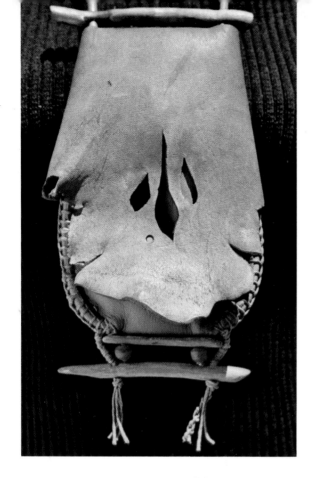

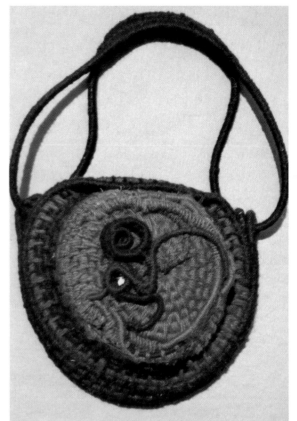

C-9
C-10

C-8

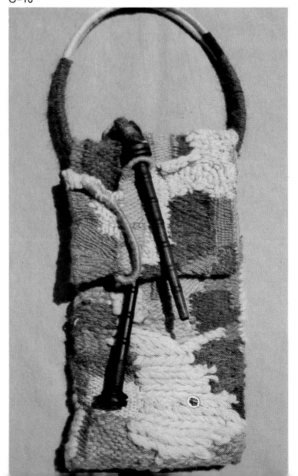

C-11

C-12

C-13

C-14

C-15

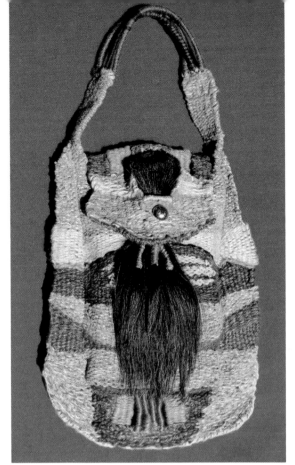

C-16

C-18
C-19

C-17

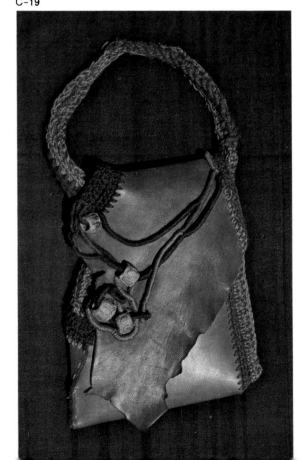

THE BAG BOOK

Lois Ericson & Diane Ericson

VNR

VAN NOSTRAND REINHOLD COMPANY
New York Cincinnati Toronto London Melbourne

For instructions on how to make the bags shown in color at
the beginning of this book, please consult the following
pages:

Copyright © 1976 by Litton Educational Publishing, Inc.
Library of Congress Catalog Card Number 75-36117
ISBN 0-442-22326-9 (cloth)
ISBN 0-442-22327-7 (paper)

Designed by Loudan Enterprises
All photographs by Moss Photography unless otherwise credited

Published in 1976 by Van Nostrand Reinhold Company
A Division of Litton Educational Publishing, Inc.
450 West 33rd Street
New York, NY 10001

Van Nostrand Reinhold Limited
1410 Birchmount Road
Scarborough, Ontario M1P 2E7, Canada

Van Nostrand Reinhold Australia Pty. Ltd.
17 Queen Street
Mitcham, Victoria 3132, Australia

Van Nostrand Reinhold Company Ltd.
Molly Millars Lane
Wokingham, Berkshire, England

16 15 14 13 12 11 10 9 8 7 6 5 4 3 2 1

Library of Congress Cataloging in Publication Data

Ericson, Lois.
    The bag book.

    Bibliography: p.
    Includes index.
    1. Handbags. 2. Textile crafts. 3. Leather
work. 4. Basket making. I. Ericson, Diane, joint
author. II. Title.
TT667.E74   646.4'8   75-36117
ISBN 0-442-22326-9
ISBN 0-442-22327-7 pbk.

Also by the author: *Shaped Weaving* (with Nik Krevitsky)

Contents

Acknowledgments

We wish to thank the artists who so generously
contributed their ideas. We owe a very
special thanks to Elmer Moss, a San Francisco
photographer, who so willingly gave his
time and professional talents to provide us with
beautiful photographs. All the photographs,
unless otherwise credited, are by Mr. Moss.

Introduction

A purse or a carryall is basically a utilitarian object used to transport articles, but it can also be a beautiful statement. Bags became popular for everyday wear around 1910, taking the strain off well-worn pockets. With the advent of mass production, the average consumer had to make do with a stamped-out product. Today the trend is toward individual style and aesthetic functional objects. In line with this trend we present this workbook of ideas to help you use your own creative energy. This is a beginning!

1

Fabric

A unique personal carryall can be made easily and with only a few sewing skills. Fabrics are readily available by the yard, and more exciting results can often be obtained by recycling used materials. Choosing your materials is your first creative decision. Fabrics, of all the materials you can use, probably have the greatest range of possibilities.

EQUIPMENT

The joy of working with fabric, in addition to its durability and washability, is the fact that very few tools are needed. A minimal but sufficient tool kit should include: scissors, tape measure, straight pins, and needle. A sewing machine is a useful option.

MATERIALS

Almost any fabric can be used to make a pocketbook: some appropriate suggestions are lightweight canvas, upholstery fabric, duck, Kettlecloth (a polyester-and-cotton blend), linen, velveteen, and corduroy. If the fabric has little or no body, such as silk or rayon, an underlining and a lining should be considered. The materials in discarded items or in little-used household linens could be the starting point for a new bag. Every material has its own unique properties, so the creative experience is always new.

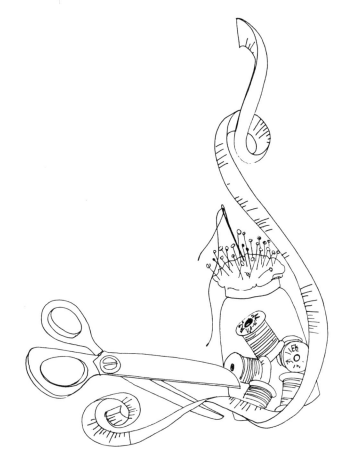

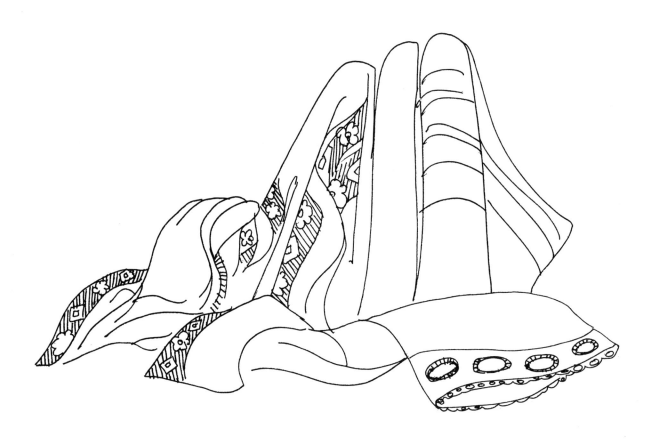

PRINTING

Printing right on your fabric is a quick, easy method of adding instant color to a bag.

Equipment: 12″ (or larger) piece of glass, Popsicle stick or brayer (inking roller), acrylic paint (at least two colors).

Materials: fabrics such as duck, canvas, cotton suedecloth, or no-wale corduroy.

Method: cut the fabric into the desired shape for the container, so you can place the design easily.

1. Squeeze the paint onto the glass.
2. Use the stick or brayer to spread the paint over the glass surface.
3. Place the fabric, right side up, on top of the paint and press to adhere the paint to the fabric.
4. Remove the fabric carefully and allow to dry for one hour (or until dry). Now the fabric is ready to be sewn up into the design of your choice.

The design on this olive-green tote has been printed.

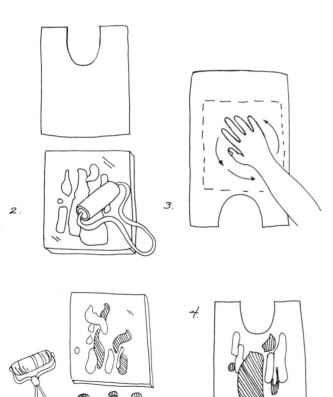

The pockets are the cutouts from the top of the bag. Both pockets and top are bound with seam binding.

TRAPUNTO

Trapunto is a quilting process. Two layers of fabric, with a polyester stuffing in between, are stitched together. The stitching, which can be done by hand or machine, may be simple or in very intricate designs. Almost any plain or printed fabric can be used; tie-dyed or batiked materials are also very handsome.

Method: this is the procedure for making the trapunto bag shown in the photograph.

1. Have ready (a) lining with stuffing and (b) batik fabric, both of which should measure 12″ × 24″.
2. (a) Put the fabric on top and pin in place; (b) shows a side view.
3. Stitch the design by hand or machine.
4. Hem or bind the raw edges with bias binding. Fold the piece in half, right sides together, and stitch the sides together.
5. Turn the fabric to the right side and attach the handle. Sea grass is used here, but cords or narrow rope would be a good substitute. Sew a small strip of fabric over the sea grass on the handle grips.

This trapunto is a cotton batik that has been machine-stitched. Shades of yellow and orange were stitched to an apple-green underlayer, which became the lining. The handles are sea grass and were sewn to the bag with orange yarn.

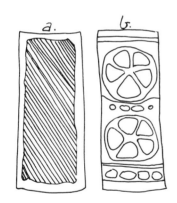

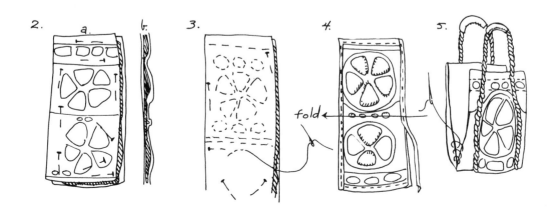

TIE-DYEING

Beautiful and varied fabrics can be made with this technique.

Materials: fabrics of natural fibers such as cotton or silk dye best. Blends of polyester or other man-made fibers require a special dye, so read the label on the dye package carefully to make sure it is acceptable. Cushings dyes were used for the examples in this book, but Ciba or procion dyes are also good. Any strong thread, cord, or yarn can be used to tie the sections of fabric. If a cold-water dye is used, rubber bands can be wrapped tightly instead of the cord. If the area to resist the dye is large, cut a strip of plastic the right size and tie the cord over it.

Method: tie-dye, as the name implies, is a method in which a fabric is tied, then dyed. The tying covers the areas that are to remain the original color. Wet the tied fabric and dye it the desired color. Then rinse the fabric thoroughly and dry. If another color is to be applied on top of the first, leave the original ties on and add the additional tying. These additional ties cover the first color so that it is retained in the end result. Rewet the fabric and dye the second color. The results of tie-dyeing are unpredictable—each piece is different. When the ties are cut off, there are always surprises. It is a good idea to choose colors that will blend together nicely in case they overlap. Here are some pattern suggestions for tie-dyeing.

1. Pick up fabric sections and wrap string around them to make circular shapes. Note: a bead, seed, or marble can be wrapped inside if desired.
2. Wrap the string around several times and tie securely.
3. The result is a sunburst type of design.

1. Pleat the material to make long folds of color.
2. Tie securely with string at both ends.
3. The result is a pattern of rectangular or square shapes, usually irregular.

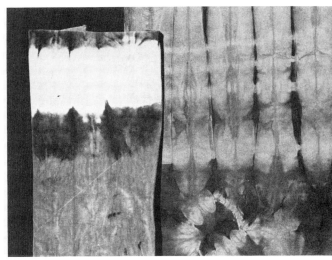

LINING

Most purses should be lined for the sake of longer wear and added stability. The lining can be subtle, matching, or contrasting. Whatever your choice, it should have body, such as denim, duck, Kettlecloth, or light canvas. This weight usually eliminates the need for interfacing. If the top of your container needs stiffening, dressmaker's buckram is good.

Method: here's how to make a lining. In fact, a lining doesn't have to be a lining at all: it can be the principal "container" of your bag. That is, the outer fabric need not be sewn together at all. What a great idea! Of course, the lining would have to be very sturdy and tacked firmly at the top of the container. This approach could lead to some wonderful designs.

1. Cut the fabric twice as long as the length of the purse plus 3″ and as wide (flat) plus 1″ for the seam allowance.
2. Fold the fabric in half and stitch both sides together.
3. You can make a pocket by cutting the fabric 6″ (or more) longer than needed and folding it as shown. The pocket is formed by sewing the sides together.
4. Turn in 1½″ at the top of the lining, pin to the purse, and tack in place.

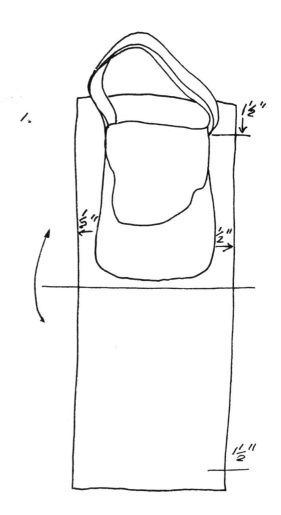

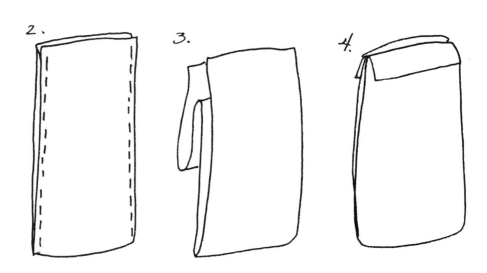

MITERED CORNERS

Method: it's easy to make a squared bottom on any bag or lining.

1. Fold the fabric in half. Decide on the width of the base and divide this measurement in half. On the right side of the material baste or insert pins on this "line." For example, if the base is to be 2" wide, baste or pin 1" from the folded edge of the material.
2. Turn the material wrong side out and stitch each side.
3. Turn right side out and you will have a perfect squared base.

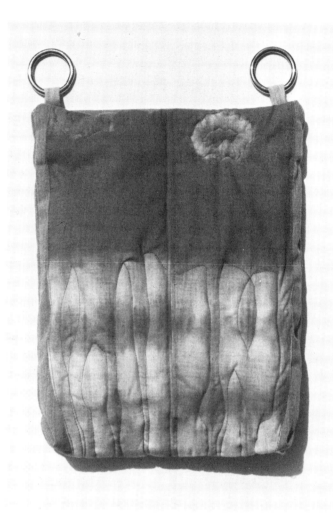

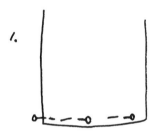

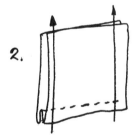

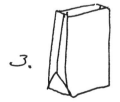

DESIGN IDEAS

This bike bag has two interchangeable straps that convert easily from short, for the handlebars, to long, for the shoulder. Velcro is stitched to each end of both sets of straps. The bag is made of Kettlecloth, and an old-fashioned bicycle is appliquéd on the front of the pocket.

Made by Colleen Miner.

The front panel of this tote bag is a danger flag from a lumberyard. There is a layer of polyester stuffing between the flag and the lining. A quilted effect is obtained by stitching around the letters.

14

Fabric, rope, and a minimum of stitching make this great carryall. The "newspaper pouch" is made of a washable polyester-and-cotton blend with a recycled rope handle. The simple design can be easily adapted to fit any size. See chapter 7 for more complete instructions.

An ordinary grocery bag is the inspiration for this picnic tote. The color is tan with red appliqué and stitching.

Modeled by Diane Ericson.

Made by Colleen Miner.

A travel bag made of denim is lined with red linen. The lining has pockets of all sizes designed to hold belongings for an overnight or weekend outing. The outside pockets on each side are just right for an extra pair of shoes or some reading material. The drawing shows a detail of the closure. A simple handle is sewn in place, and a 72" zipper is stitched all around. The overall dimensions are 22" × 28".

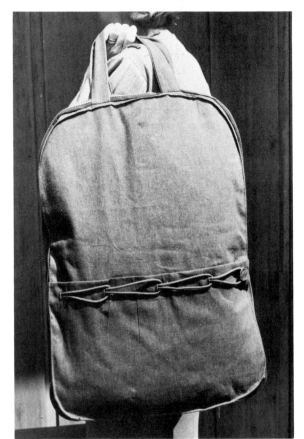

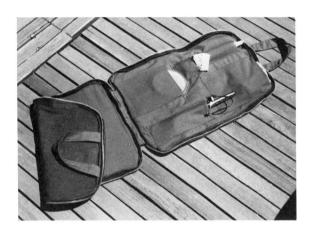

1. Vertical buttonholes are made in the pocket.
2. Loops of rayon cording are cut twice as long as the space between the buttonholes plus 2". For example, if the space is 4", the cording should be 4" × 2 = 8" + 2 = 10". The loops are stitched to the body of the purse in line with the buttonholes.
3. To fasten the pocket, pull each loop through the facing buttonhole and "button" to the next loop. Fasten the last loop to a button.

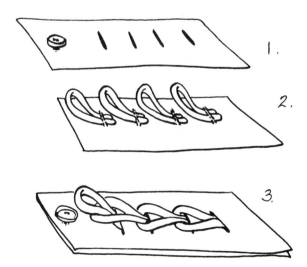

1.

2.

3.

Have a picnic in style with this contemporary lunchtime tote. It is made of sturdy-weight canvas, and the edges of all the pockets are stitched flat with seam tape. Compartments for favorite foods and drink are labeled in Swedish with letters stenciled in blue acrylic paint. The handles are clothes hangers from an old trunk.

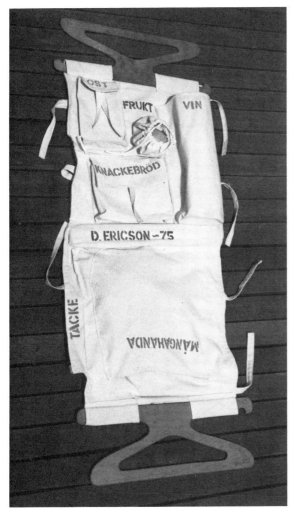

A casual tote is made of heavy white cotton. The tucked design was inspired by lines on snow-covered hillsides. The tucks were sewn with rust-colored thread. The handle is coiled with rust-colored rug wool. See chapter 5 for coiling instructions.

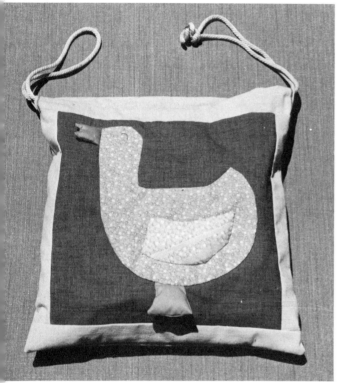

Made by Colleen Miner.

A patchwork duck decorates this child's bag on one side. On the other side is an identification label in the form of a letter complete with a stamp, stating the owner's residence. A cotton-rope drawstring is strung through a casing at the top.

A personalized schoolbag in washable cotton is embroidered with animals drawn by the proud owner.

Made by Kristine Barrett and modeled by Stevie Barrett.

Cotton fabric makes a lightweight, comfortable backpack. The doily-and-flowered-gingham appliqué adds a very feminine touch.

Made and modeled by Colleen Miner.

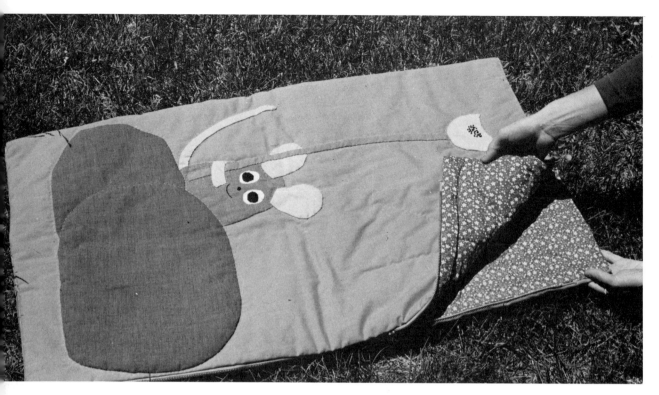

Made by Colleen Miner.

This child's sleeping bag is inspired by Leo Leoni's book *Frederick.* The mouse, rocks, and flowers are appliqués. The bag is quilted and has a zipper on one side and across the bottom to open flat.

This tote bag is made of pieced knit fabric in warm colors. The stitches used in the design are Cretan, chain, and French knots. There is corded welting between the gusset and the front and back.

Made by Linda Edison.

Elegant white silk is lavishly appliquéd with doilies and pieces of handmade lace. The small crocheted ovals attached to the corners harmonize with the bag. The closure is expandable metal.

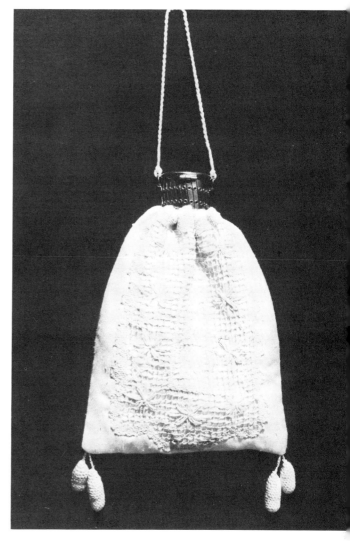

Made by Jonda Friel.

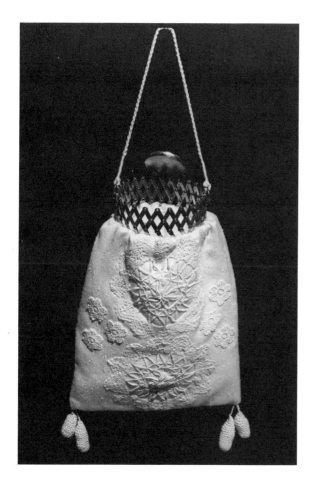

Sand-colored cotton suedecloth is the fabric here. Tie-dye is used to create the design on the material, and the design is enhanced with trapunto stitching.

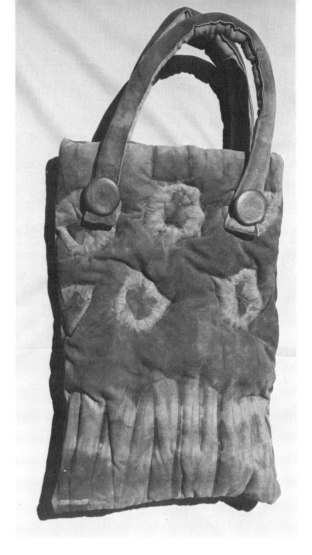

Pieces of sheepskin in various shades of brown are sewn together to make a hand container. The muff has a zipper as the closure on the pocket, shown open.

Made by Colleen Miner.

A beach bag, made of natural canvas, is printed with acrylic paint. The shapes are formed by stamping blocks of wood, a cup, and pencil erasures into the paint, then onto the fabric.

A flower design on needlepoint canvas is the focal point of this petite, colorful purse. The main body of the bag is lightweight upholstery fabric, color-coordinated to enhance the stitchery. The edges are cotton cable cord in the same fabric. The wooden handles are a pleasing contrast.

Made by Linda Edison.

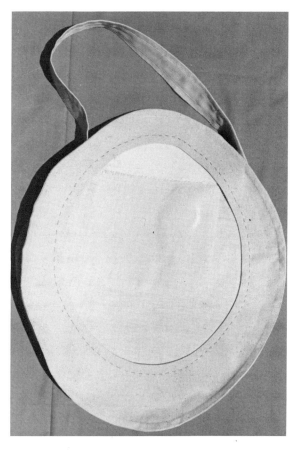

This purse is a "frame" in which the "picture" can be changed. The fabric is natural canvas. There are three main pieces: the front with the cutout, the back, and the gusset-handle. Each section is lined and completely finished. The pieces are then stitched together. Several insets could be made to change as desired. Some possibilities for a centerpiece are weaving, appliqué, or stitching (as in the bag above). The completed bag is shown in Chapter 2.

This front-pack has a hand-painted art-nouveau-inspired design outlined with stitchery. The fabric for this front pack is cotton, painted with acrylic and embroidered with perle cotton. Silver contact paper was fastened to heavy cardboard and placed behind the oval cutout. The cutout and edges were bound with seam binding. The bag has a side zipper and straps that cross and tie in back. This is a great style for people in wheelchairs.

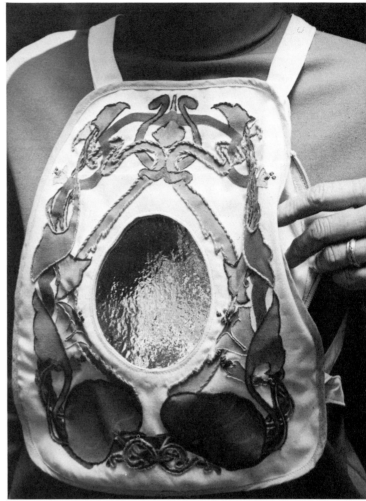

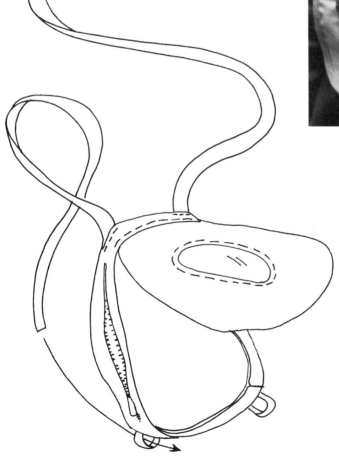

Collection of Gayle Luchessa.

24

Blue denim is the durable fabric used for this bag. The handles and top are cut from a piece of latigo leather. The pocket "hole" is cut out of the leather, and the fabric is fastened on the wrong side. The selvage edges are sewn to the right side to add a decorative note.

Burnt-orange upholstery fabric is highlighted with strips of black leather and horsehair sewn in place. The handle is lined with black leather. The ornament is a brass doorknob.

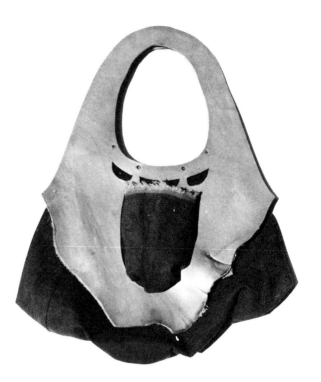

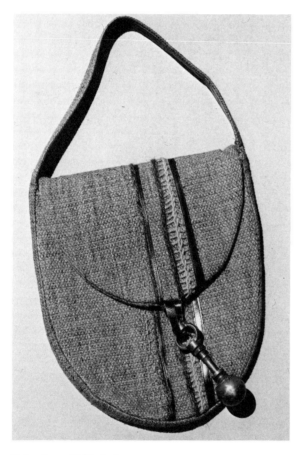

Collection of Lois Bailey.

Corded cotton in a dark red shade is the fabric for this bag. The bag is fastened to the coiled handles with tabs of fabric. The tabs are stitched to the bag over the handle, then to the lining. The coiled handles are shown in chapter 5.

If you want to be a sensation on the courts, appear carrying this yellow canvas tennis-racket case. Functional as well as entertaining, this sturdy bag will carry your tennis balls to Wimbledon!

An old fabric backpack given new life. Two changeable flaps are painted, embroidered, and appliquéd. Velcro tabs are sewn to the bag and to the back of the flaps. Two bags in one!

Made by Georgeann Rees.

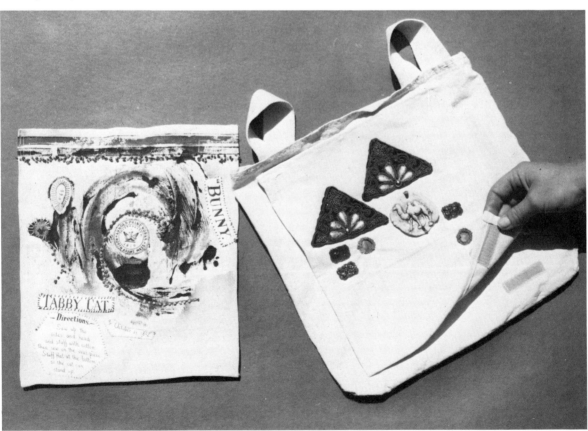

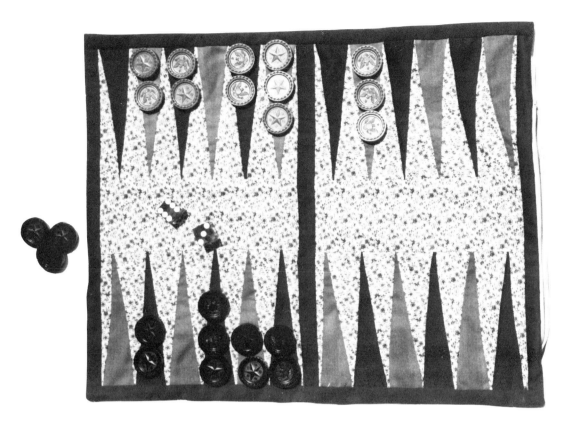

Made by Colleen Miner.

Backgammon and checkers to take along on a trip or hike. The designs are appliquéd in cotton fabric.

Stitchery, bits of fur, and a few beads enhance this wool purse. The handles are wrapped with both smooth and nubby yarns for an interesting effect.

Beige polyester gabardine is the fabric in this simple, yet elegant bag. The trim is finger-woven linen bands with brass bells.

Made by Bets Barnard.

Knit fabric is combined with a crocheted panel in this small bag. The fabric snaps to the wooden handles, so the body of the bag could be changed.

Made by Kristine Barrett.

2
Weaving

Weaving is an ancient craft, one that has seen many revisions and applications. Even now weaving is constantly taking on new dimensions. Utilizing a variety of simple techniques and equipment, it will be easy for you to express a unique style in a personal carryall.

EQUIPMENT

The equipment you will need to start with is minimal and easily accessible: a frame, picture frame, or canvas-stretcher bars and finishing nails (optional); or sturdy cardboard, slightly larger than the pattern, and straight pins or bank pins. You should also have scissors, a small beater or table fork, and a yarn needle (a curved tip is desirable).

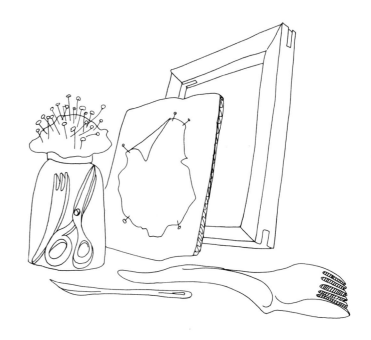

MATERIALS

The warp threads are the basic foundation to weave through, usually lengthwise. The thread should be strong and firm (one that won't stretch), such as cotton carpet warp, crochet cotton, perle cotton, or linen. If the warp threads are not to be included in the design, choose a color that will blend with the weft threads.

The weft threads cross the warp to make the cloth. Almost all yarns or fibers can be used: a variety of textures and hues will make your project more interesting. Other materials such as beads or wooden buttons can be inserted for ornament. Additional decorating ideas and materials are described in chapter 6.

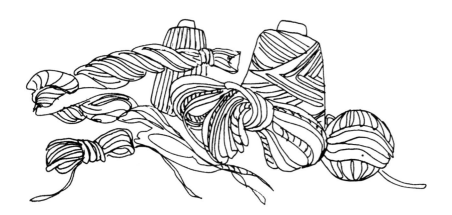

PIN WEAVING

Pin weaving is one of the most versatile weaving methods because almost any shape can be created. As a base for the weaving use a piece of heavy cardboard, a cardboard box, or fiberboard.

Method: make a paper pattern and either draw the design on the board or lay it down and pin it in place.

1. To fasten the warp, insert the straight pins at a very low angle to the cardboard. Place the pins ⅛″ to ¼″ apart. If you are using fine weft threads to make a detailed design, the warps should be close together. For a thicker weft use a wider spacing.

2. Make an open slip knot and fasten it to the first pin. It is best to insert the pins as you wind the warp on. When you have warped the entire pattern shape, fasten the warp thread to the last pin with an open slip knot. This completes the warp.

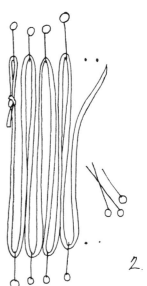

If the warp is to show, use a single or thin thread. If the warp is to be completely covered, use a doubled or thick yarn. Thread the yarn needle and start weaving over and under the threads. Start a new thread 1″ or 2″ in from the edge of the warp, then continue weaving to the edge and return. This assures a smooth selvage. The first and last rows next to the pins have to be done very carefully. The needle and thread must pass *between* warp threads on each pin. It is wise to weave the ends by the pins first.

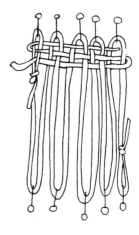

The weft should be packed firmly, which is usually done with a beater. A table fork or comb can also be used. To keep the edges of the weaving straight, you have to "bubble" the weft as it is inserted. This also makes it easier to cover the warp completely. As the weft is woven across, lay it in rather loosely in an arc, then make several smaller arcs and beat with the beater.

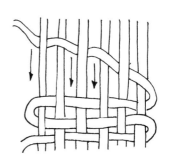

FRAME-LOOM WEAVING

An excellent loom can be made from an old picture frame or canvas stretcher. Simply hammer small finishing nails to the front of the frame ¼" apart. The warp is put on the loom in the same way as in pin weaving. It can also be wrapped around and around, in which case the purse is woven in a tubular form, eliminating the side seams. As with pin weaving, decide on a design, choose the fibers, and proceed with the technique.

BASIC WEAVES

Tabby or plain weave is the basic weave. A single thread proceeds over, then under one warp thread at a time. It is a balanced weave: just as much of the warp thread shows as the weft.

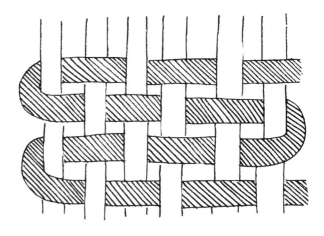

A tapestry weave covers the warp completely. Use a doubled or heavy yarn and proceed over and under two warp threads at a time. Pack the weft threads firmly with a beater.

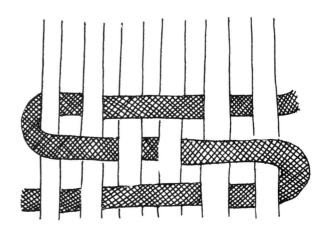

A soumak weave is great for adding variety and texture. It is done as an outline stitch in embroidery, treating the warp threads as a fabric. Here are two ways to make the stitch: (1) across three and back around two threads or (2) across two and back around one. After you have completed one row, weave a tabby row to return, then proceed with another row of soumak.

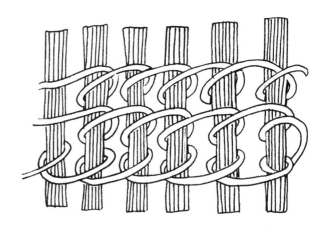

A rya knot creates a shag effect. Use four or more strands of yarn. Start by inserting a needle between two threads, pointing the needle to the left. As the threads are pulled, let the end extend as long as the fringe is to be. Then bring the thread around in a circle and pick up the right-hand warp, proceeding from the right back to the center. Pull down tight to make the knot.

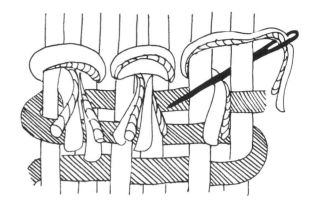

Loops create a nice texture without using any particular weave. Simply lay in a plain-weave row and pull up a loop here and there across the warp. This should be done in a random pattern for interest and to ensure a solid weave.

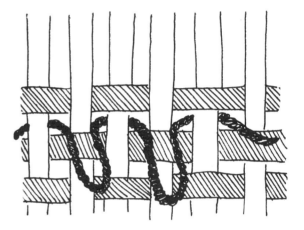

Slits are vertical openings that are formed when a weft thread proceeding from one side stops at a certain point in the weave and returns to the same side. The weft from the other side comes to the same point and returns to its side without crossing a common warp thread.

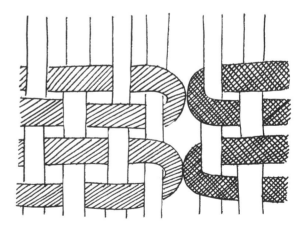

Sections of a weaving can be padded so that some shapes in the design are rounded. This is accomplished by basting a piece of fabric to the back and stuffing it.

Extra warps can be added by cutting additional warp threads in the desired lengths and looping them around the original warp threads. The cut ends should be pinned for tension and woven, and the ends wrapped.

An interesting way to finish thread ends is achieved by wrapping the last 2" or more instead of weaving them. The resulting loops can be used to attach the handles or embellish the design.

If your loom is small but the area to be covered is large, consider appliquéing a woven section that can be spread apart to fit a large area. Make slits in the fabric as the weaving progresses.

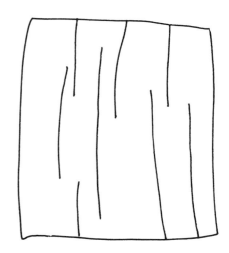

When the weaving is removed from the loom, it can easily be stretched into any horizontal shape.

In this example the leather is cut to make warp "threads." The slits are pinned to a piece of cardboard to create enough tension for easy weaving. Leather strips and various yarns, including a few precious handspuns, are woven together to create a pleasing effect.

DESIGN IDEAS

This beach bag is made of pillow ticking. The blue-and-white ticking is cut in 1″ strips, leaving the raw edges. To weave the strips together, they are placed on top of layers of red cotton and lightweight canvas. All three layers are stitched together with red thread. The handle is also make of ticking, which is folded and stitched. The red cotton and the canvas (lining) are sewn together to make a tube for a dowel, which keeps the top rigid.

Two prints, with similar colors, are used quite effectively in this example. The back shows how to sew the strips down after weaving them together. The edges of the strips are left unfinished. With a little additional work the edges could be finished by cutting them wider, turning the edges under, and pressing in place.

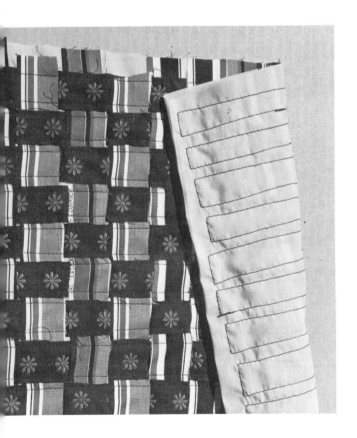

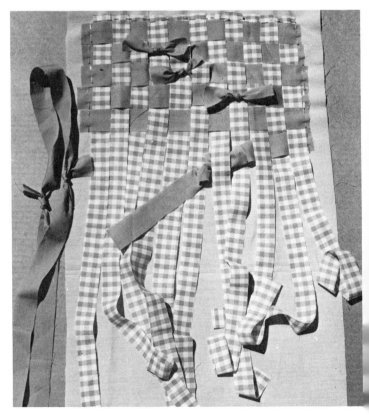

The checked strips are the warp. The plain strips are knotted together for texture and as a substitute for sewing. The knots are formed in a random pattern.

A yardage-bolt cardboard is the base for this long woven bag. The stitches used are tabby and soumak. The flap was folded over twice and stitched to make a pocket for sunglasses. It is fastened and decorated with antique wooden bobbins. The handles are made from two rows of wrapped cord fastened together.

The drawing shows how the ready-made cardboard form is warped for this purse. It is woven as a tube, so there are no side seams to sew up.

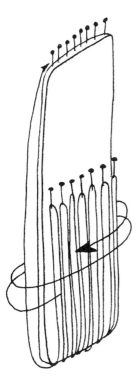

This small shag purse is woven in squares, then assembled. The wool yarn, in many shades of green, is woven in the rya technique. The hat-shaped pouch is trimmed with crochet at the sides, which pulls it together and forms loops to fasten the handles to the bag.

This photograph shows a pin-weaving warp set up on a cardboard loom. A paper pattern was cut out and drawn on the cardboard. Almost any shape is possible, so be creative!

Purple, lavender, royal blue, and white yarns are used to make the cover of this bag. A strip of wood is inserted inside (at the fold) to stiffen the cover. The sides are folded around to the back, overlapped, and stitched.

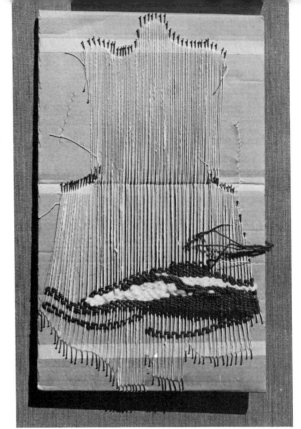

The pouch was made with dark blue cotton. A rope, wrapped with blue yarn, is attached for a handle. See chapter 4 for details on attaching handles. By experimenting with various materials, one basic pattern could be adapted to several functional containers.

The front panel for this belt pouch is pin weaving. The design is woven with thin wool yarn. The back, also woven, has a zipper closure. This small oval pouch is fastened to an art-nouveau clip that slides on a belt. It would be a nice accessory to wear with a long skirt.

The pattern for the shape and design of the belt pouch is fastened to a piece of cardboard. Dark wine wool is accentuated with shades of periwinkle blue, green, and yellow.

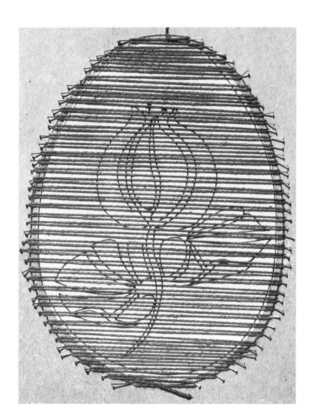

Chenille yarn was used to weave this purse, giving it an elegant appearance. The colors are soft yellow and green. The handles are coiled. Coiling is explained in chapter 5.

Red, fuchsia, and wine wool combine with cut strips of velvet to make an elegant evening bag.

The tapestry is attached to an old silver purse top. The opened purse shows the silk lining in vibrant pink, red, white, and navy.

This neck pouch was made from part of a Mexican belt. The sides are sewn, and several strands of yarn are fastened to the purse. The strands are knotted in a simple overhand knot and wrapped on each side of the knot. The pouch can be tied either around the neck or around the waist. The fringe is also wrapped.

A belt purse is made by combining a small tapestry with no-wale corduroy. The colors are various shades of gold with hot-pink accents. The top that becomes the loop for the belt is also the flap to cover the opening.

This belt pouch is woven in a rya stitch. It is pin-woven on a cardboard loom, and the strap is crocheted.

The next three bags are made entirely of rag strips, a great recycling idea. This white-and-natural bag is woven with a cardboard-box loom. The wrapping on the flap end of the warp is a good way to finish the edge. Sea-lion and boar teeth are sewn in place for ornament. The handle is doubled over for extra padding and comfort.

Sand and red cotton strips, cut 1″ wide, are the warp and weft in this bag. The warp "threads" were tied together and pinned to a piece of cardboard. The knotted warps were left as is to provide a simple ending for the flap. The handle is coiled (see chapter 5).

Different shades of red rags are loom-woven together on a red and purple wool warp. Crocheted trim is applied. The driftwood handles, stained brown with shoe dye, are also crocheted in place.

This bag started from one long, rather plain rectangle of weaving. When the fabric was removed from the loom, sections of it were stuffed, then stitched. A strip cut from the side of the rectangle was sewn into a tube and padded for the handle, which makes a very comfortable shoulder strap.

Shades of fuchsia and red enfold strips of brown fur in this wintery bag. The handle is a tube, which should be stuffed lightly for comfort if it is to be worn on the shoulder. The dimensions of the main body of this purse are 12″ square. Note: To use fur, always cut from the back (the skin side) with a razor blade or sharp knife.

This classic white bag is a study in texture. The warp, which also becomes the fringe, is linen. It is wrapped and knotted to finish the ends. The ornament is a silver art-nouveau buckle. A pair of tubes fastened together becomes the handle.

Finger-woven strips are sewn together to make a colorful purse. The strap is also finger weaving. The unwoven yarn at the ends of the bands becomes the fringe. The wrapping at the top of the bag creates a handsome effect, and a traditional loop and button closure adds interest.

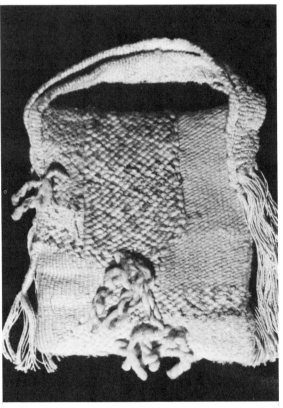

Made by Jonda Friel.

46

This large oval pin weaving measures 12" × 15". Various weights of yarn, fabric strips, and string combine to make a pleasing inset for the canvas "frame."

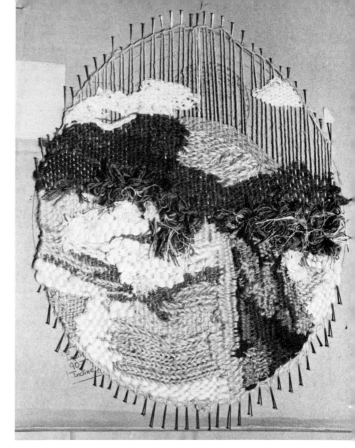

The background for this purse is a "frame" of canvas, stitched together with a gusset, which becomes the handle, set in the side. The pin weaving is then set into the center and tacked in place.

Several inset pieces could be made and changed with your mood. Simply baste or tack the choice for the day in place. This one is made of leather shapes and glued together with leather glue. It is sewn to a piece of fabric for easy insertion into the "frame."

A contemporary Indian pouch is decorated with a horsetail and a silver moccasin button. The colors in this imaginative bag are beige, brown, and gold, with turquoise accents.

The basic shape is woven in one piece, then folded and sewn together. The warp threads on the strap end are tied and wrapped. To balance the visual weight of the horsetail, an additional pin weaving is sewn to the outside edge.

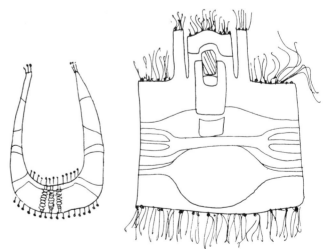

Shades of blue, brown, and dusty rose are woven on a shaped cardboard loom. The warp is pinned at the top. The threads are wrapped starting from a pin on the front side, then moving under the back, around the next pin, and back and forth until the entire width is warped. The handles are pieces of wood fastened together with screws.

Yellow suede strips are knotted together and laid in (as yarn) to create a great texture. This bag is loom-woven with a warp of yellow and brown shades. The handles are made with a woven strip held on by brass rings sewn to each side.

This bag is woven on a frame loom. The rectangle is then sewn together on the sides. The finger-woven handle is attached to the sides, and the ends are finished with handsome silver tubes.

A black purse with gray and white accents that repeat the shapes of chain mail. The stainless-steel chain mail was originally part of a slaughterhouse apron. The side panel has an inset of wrapping that continues around the top to form the handle.

Made by Jonda Friel.

A rectangular shape of pin weaving is appliquéd onto a crocheted tube. The slits in the weaving are spread and manipulated to show the underlayer. The handle is an old Japanese cavalry bit combined with wrapping.

This tubular bag, of natural wool with a dark brown stripe, is loom-woven and then hand-sewn onto the leather top. The brown leather top is riveted together. The strap, also riveted, slides through slits in the top.

Made by Bets Barnard.

This knitting bag is based on a traditional Liberian rice bag. The technique is similar to finger-weaving worked in the round. The handles are rattan, and the bag is lined with canvas.

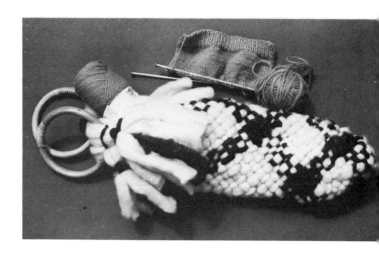

A knitting reticule made by sewing finger-woven bands together. The yarn is fastened to the wooden handle with a knot.

Made by Jackie Wollenberg.

Collection of Lilly Carlson.

Shades of rose, wine, lavender, and dark blue combine beautifully in this saddlebag. A 12″ × 28″ rectangle of a Swedish goathair-and-wool blend is woven for each end of the bag.

52

In this bag rectangles are folded in half, and the sides are stitched together. The center section was left unwoven to incorporate sprang and plaiting. This bag was inspired by a similar double bag from Guatemala.

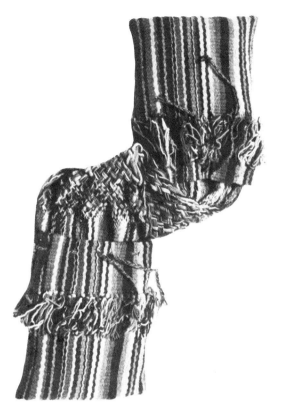

A linen card weaving becomes the gusset (flat) and the handle (tubular) on this handsome tote bag. The weft for the card weaving becomes the warp for the sprang on the side panels. The top of the sprang is wrapped. The bag is lined to support the open weave.

Made by Jackie Wollenberg.

This wool-and-linen backpack was warped on a picture frame and woven in a single piece. There is a vertical zipper on the back so the design on the front is uninterrupted.

3
Crochet

Crochet has taken on a new look—it has become a sculptural form. *Any* shape is a possibility. Instead of following a repetitious pattern, experimenting with just a few simple stitches will make crocheting really fun.

EQUIPMENT

The equipment needed for crocheting is minimal—just a hook and some yarn or string. If your hook is fairly small, it may be held like a pencil. If it is medium or large, it is easier to grasp overhand like a steering wheel. To choose the right size hook, put the yarn over the hook. If the yarn slips off too easily, the hook is too small. Crochet hooks are usually made of bone, metal, or plastic, but a wooden one is especially nice. It is a real pleasure to use a handsome tool.

MATERIALS

The materials, as always, are the prime consideration. The yarn should be sturdy and long-wearing, such as wool rug yarn, goat-hair, horsehair, jute (make sure it is colorfast), coarse synthetic blends, or cotton cord. If the yarn is thin, use it double.

ORNAMENTATION

The flap is the point of greatest creativity in crochet. To add interest to the front of a purse, consider attaching an ornament. Some suggestions are: metal buttons, seed pods, pieces of driftwood, buckles, or beads. Whatever you choose should correspond with the handles in material, color, or "feeling." Ornaments give weight to the flap in addition to decorating it.

HANDLES

Crocheted handles are probably the first idea that comes to mind, but consider other alternatives—bamboo, rattan, tortoise, wood, metal (such as horse bits), driftwood, bones, rope, or leather strips. Some of the most interesting possibilities for a handle come from unexpected sources. One good idea is to look for handles on discarded handbags in second-hand stores.

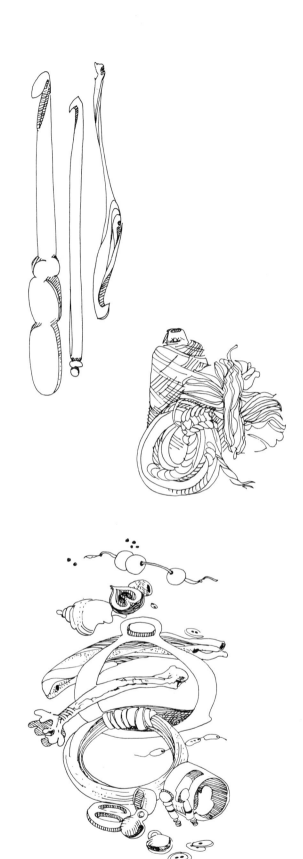

BASIC STITCHES

Make a slip knot (1) to begin, then a chain stitch (2). To make a chain stitch, pass your hook to the left, put the yarn over the hook, and pull it through the loop that is formed, thus making a second loop. Hold the yarn in whatever way is comfortable for you, maintaining some tension on the yarn to keep a degree of uniformity in the stitches. Make the chain stitches quite loose so that it will be easy to do the succeeding rows. This is one point to stress right at the beginning: "stay loose." If you are tense, your project becomes difficult.

After you have completed about 1' of chain, try single crochet stitches (1). Leave one chain stitch at the end of the yarn as the work is turned to keep the row as wide at the beginning as at the end. Insert the hook into the second chain, put the yarn over the hook, and pull it through the chain. This leaves two loops on the hook. Yarn-over again and pull through both loops. You can also try some double crochet stitches (2): chain two stitches at the end of the yarn as the turn is made. To begin the double crochet stitch, first wrap the yarn around the hook. Insert the hook in the chain, put the yarn over the hook, and pull it through the chain. Now there are three loops on the hook. Yarn-over, taking off two of the loops; yarn-over again, taking off the third of the original loops and the loop created by the yarn-over. Most pattern stitches are multiples and/or combinations of these basic stitches, so keep experimenting and enjoy yourself.

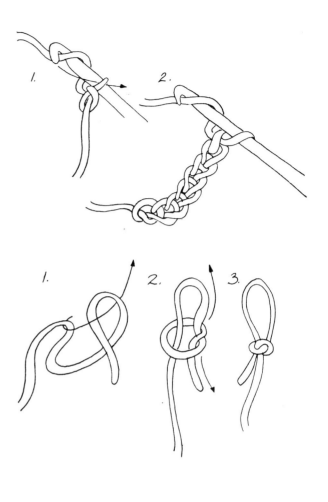

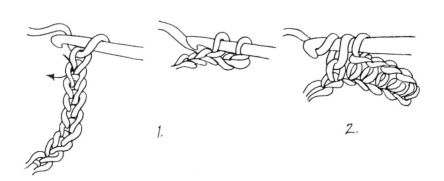

To make a piece wider or narrower, increase by making two stitches in one stitch of the previous row or decrease by making one stitch through two stitches in the previous row.

After turning on the next row and making a few stitches, make about ten chain stitches (yes, right in the middle of the row). Fasten the yarn *anywhere* in the part already completed by inserting the hook, putting the yarn over the hook, pulling up a loop, and completing the stitch. There is no need to finish the row: just continue working over the chain. To start in a new place, simply put the hook through a "hole," pull up a loop, make single or double crochet stitches, and keep working. Tubular shapes, odd-shaped "holes," or rounded shapes will soon begin to evolve. One marvelous fact about crocheting—there is only one stitch to keep track of at a time—*terrific!*

Increasing.

Decreasing.

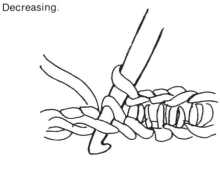

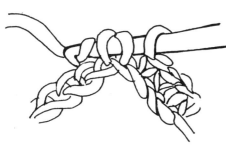

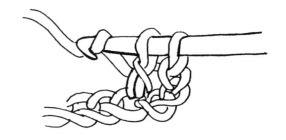

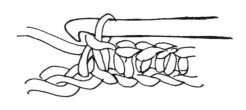

When you have practiced and experimented to your satisfaction, it is time to begin a purse. To determine the size, measure a favorite purse and note the dimensions (circumference and depth). Make a chain the circumference measurement and slip-stitch together to make a circle. Single crochet one stitch in each chain all around. Chain one stitch and proceed to the next row. Continue making rows until the desired depth is reached, using single or double crochet stitches or alternating rows.

Crochet a chain. Wooden crochet hook by Bill Horgos.

Use single or double crochet stitches (or alternate the two) until the tube is the desired depth. Leave a long piece of thread at the end to sew the bottom.

Circumference of the purse slip-stitched together.

Flatten the "tube" and either crochet, using single crochet stitches, or sew the bottom together on the wrong side.

Sew the bottom together.

To create a flap, fasten the thread at the top where the flap is to attach. Simply put the hook into a hole and the yarn over the hook and pull up a loop. The flap can also be made separately by starting with a chain and crocheting and then sewing it on later.

The purse was crocheted in this technique. The handle of the rust wool bag is a horse bit. A small piece of metal decorates the flap.

Any crochet pattern stitch for one medallion or square can be made with thick yarn and a large hook so that only two motifs are needed, for the front and the back of the purse.

Method: Here is how to make the purse shown in the photo.
Row 1: chain (ch) 4, slip-stitch (sl) tog.
Row 2: 10 single crochet (sc) in a circle.
Row 3: 2 double crochet (dc) in each sc around.
Row 4: cluster (cl)* in 1 dc, 2 dc in 1 dc around.
Row 5: 3 dc and 1 cl in each dc of the previous row, repeat.
Row 6: scallop edge: 4 dc in 1 dc of the previous row, 2 sc in the next 2 dc (treat the cluster stitch as a dc), repeat. Make two sc edges and put together. For the handle, ch 35, sc in each chain. Then sc in each sc of previous row and attach to sides.
*cluster: make 4 dc, pulling the loops *long* and each time leaving the last loop on the hook. To complete the cluster, draw a loop through all the loops at once.

Purse made of heavy white yarn by Lilly Carlson.

DESIGN IDEAS

An antique European purse top becomes the accent for this small, black crocheted evening bag. Popcorn and single crochet stitches are used. To make a popcorn stitch, make 5 dc in 1 dc of the previous row. Remove the hook from the loop and insert it in the top of the first dc. Pick up the loop from the last dc and pull it through the first dc. This creates a knob or bump that looks like popcorn. A metallic-thread appliqué is attached and crocheted at random over the bag. The handle is also single crochet, in keeping with the dainty style of the bag.

Black and brown combine nicely in this dressy bag. A discarded mouton-lamb cuff creates the top half of the purse. The bottom is crocheted of black thick-and-thin rayon yarn. A simple crocheted handle and a silver hair ornament complete the bag.

Pale green rug wool is used to make this attractive bag. The wooden handles are handmade. The beads are made of vegetable ivory and sewn in place. A little wrapping finishes the flap.

This black wool bag is made entirely of single crochet. Interest is created on the body of the bag, so a flap isn't necessary. The appliquéd leather scraps create unique negative shapes.

Rope handles that continue down onto the purse make this bag unusual. The rope is wrapped and crocheted to make a design on the front and back. The sisal rope is unraveled in some areas to provide a contrast in texture.

Soft shades of orange wool are worked in alternating rows of single and double crochet. The flap is simply decorated with a tab that extends from front to back. A silver buckle is the ornament, and a crocheted handle is attached.

Collection of Madeline Bohanon.

Lime green jute is the material used to crochet this casual bag. The handle is double crochet, and the body of the bag is single and double crochet done in random rows. Wood and jute make a nice combination. A free-form flap is enhanced with several old-fashioned clothespins and some wrapping.

Brown wool and goathair are crocheted together to create the interesting texture of this bag. The twisted rattan handles are from an old purse. Brown seed pods and wrapping complete the bag.

Collection of Helen Souza.

Crochet and leather are combined to form this feminine pouch. The style utilizes a piece of leather in its natural shape, enhancing the softness of the fabric with small tucks to give fullness. The offset handles add interest.

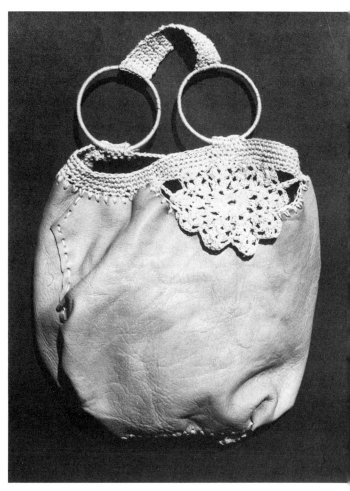

Made by Lois Sherman.

Gold jute is combined with rattan and seashells in this tubular purse. The rattan handles, used upside down, lend a unique style to the bag. The front of the bag, enhanced with shells and wrapping, is the focal point, making a flap optional.

4
Leather

Leather is a versatile and sturdy material with unlimited possibilities. It can be used quite effectively by itself or in combination with almost any fiber technique. Leather is a most handsome material for a carryall. It is easy to work with and hard-wearing, and the edges need no finishing.

EQUIPMENT

Few tools are needed to achieve very nice results. The most important is a tool to make holes. A leather punch is the best: it has a rotating head with a choice of six sizes of round holes. Punching the holes ¼" apart and ¼" from the edge of the leather is a general guide. Experiment on a scrap of leather to determine the right size of the holes and the right distance between them for your project.

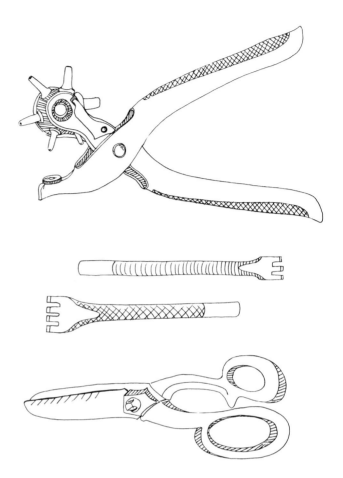

A prong chisel can also be used: it has to be pounded with a hammer, and several slits are made at one time. Again, the distance from the edge should usually be ¼" (the distance between the holes is already established). A pounding board is a thick leather board, useful in making clean-cut slits. If none of these tools is available, a hammer and nail can be used to punch holes. There is always a way!

Another good tool to have is a pair of leather scissors, which makes cutting much easier. If you plan to use a great deal of leather, it will be a good investment.

MATERIALS

There are many weights of leather available, one of which is right for almost any project. Very soft, smooth leather or suede works well with machine stitching and on small details such as gathering, pleating, tucking, and cording. Medium weights of leather can be used effectively in combination with fiber techniques or simply sewn together by themselves. They can also be used to mold leather into a desired shape. Heavy leather can be used to make interesting tops for bags.

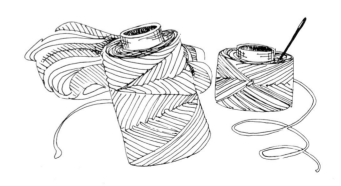

Strong stitching thread should be used, such as waxed linen or nylon upholstery thread (available in assorted colors). These are especially good to sew leather to leather. Other sewing materials to consider are wool rug yarn, linen, and thin cord. These are used when other textile techniques are used in combination with leather.

STITCHES

Many embroidery and sewing stitches can be used with leather. Two basic stitches are the most useful.

To make a back stitch, knot the thread and bring the needle through the material on the stitch line (either real or imaginary), then take a small backward stitch through the material (1). Bring the needle through the fabric again in front of the last stitch and take another backward stitch.

To make a chain stitch, knot the thread and bring the needle through the material, holding down the thread with your thumb. Insert the needle where the thread first emerged and bring the point out a short distance away, always keeping the working thread under the point of the needle (2).

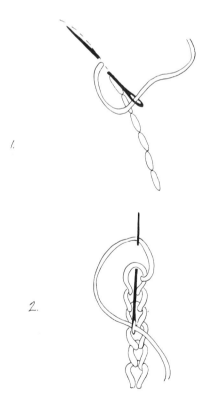

1.

2.

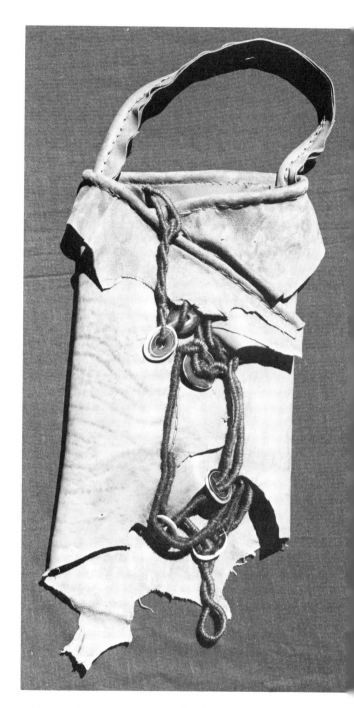

This casual bag utilizes the free-flowing edges of the leather. Polished deer-antler slices add a decorative element to the design of the purse.

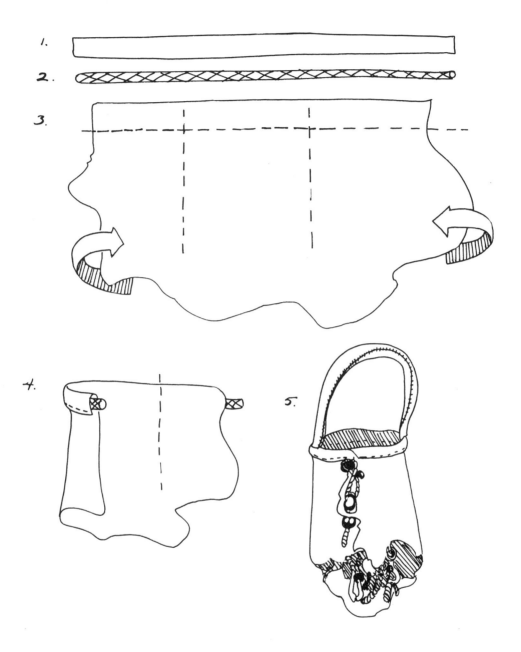

Method: the diagram above shows how to make the beautiful purse shown on page 69.

1. Cut a strip measuring 20″ × 2½″ for the handle.
2. Cut a piece of cord (upholsterers' welting or cotton cable cord) the length of the diameter of the bag.
3. Fold the purse body as indicated.
4. Fold the top edge over the welting and sew it to the body by hand. Use a soft piece of leather: a sharp needle will penetrate it easily so you won't have to punch holes.
5. Fold the sides in and sew together down the front. The extra threads, attached to the front, are wrapped. The handle can also be corded for strength. Cut a lining the dimensions of the leather. Since the lining supports the contents, it should be of durable fabric such as polyester gabardine, tacked firmly at the top to complete the bag. The outer shell need not be sewn together at the bottom. Instructions for cording and wrapping are given in chapter 6; for lining, in chapter 1.

This pigskin bag is stitched by hand through prepunched holes with linen thread. The holes are made with a slit punch. The flap here is a piece of pin weaving, but leather, crochet, or coiling can also be used. The materials used on this weaving are wool, suede strips, and linen, together with a small mirror. The handle is fitted to the style of the bag as well as to the contour of the shoulder. A ¼" hole is drilled at each end of the curved piece of wood to attach the wrapped thread for the remainder of the handle. Loops of leather are sewn on the sides of the bag to attach the wrapping. Instructions for inserting mirrors and wrapping are given in chapter 6.

Method: the drawing shows how to assemble the pieces of leather.

1. A and B are the side pieces, and C is the loops for the handles.
2. Stitch front, sides, and bottom together. Stitch the pocket to the front piece. Stitch the front (with pocket) to the side and bottom pieces. Stitch the front with the sides to the back piece.
3. The flap can be left plain or woven with decorative additions. The handles can be a combination of materials such as wood, rope, and leather.

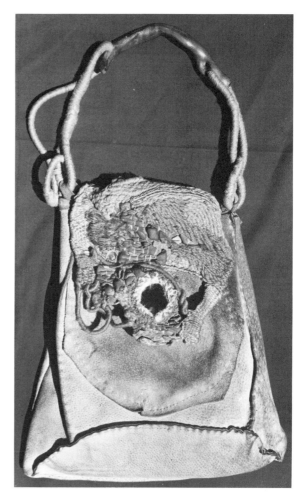

Leather, yarns, and driftwood create a pleasing effect in this shoulder bag.

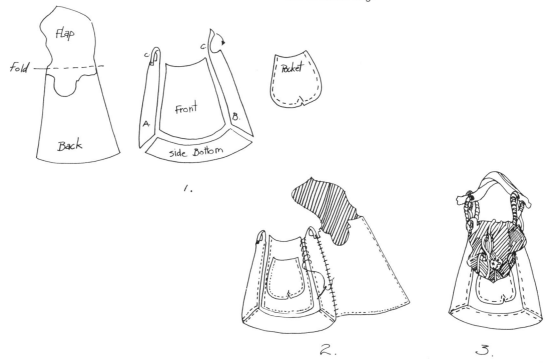

DESIGN IDEAS

Soft yellow suede is corded and tucked to make this elegant evening bag. The cording and the tucking are done first, then the desired shape is cut out. The sides and bottom are simply sewn together. The bag is unlined. The top is antique gold with amethysts. The handle is a gold watch chain.

This warm brown cowhide bag has a woven accent. A gusset, sewn on the sides and bottom, is extended to make the handle. The handle is hand-stitched for a handsome effect. A small tapestry section is placed behind the cutout of a bird. The leather is cut to simulate feathers. The appliqué is attached to a suede lining on the side of the bag behind the weaving. The overall dimensions are 16″ × 28″.

Made by Diane Snyder.

A piece of red leather is used here in its original shape: that is, it is not cut. Holes are punched on the sides to be sewn together and filled in with crocheting. Single crochet is the only stitch used. Wrapping is added to the flap, and stoneware beads are attached with the wrapping.

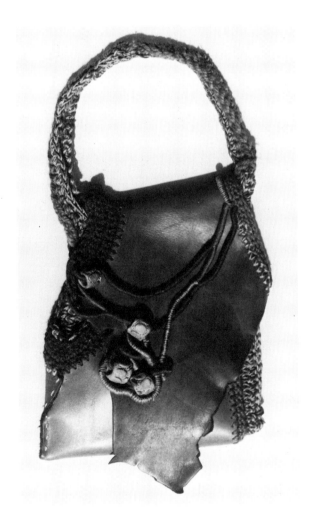

This neutral leather carryall is trimmed with interlaced pieces of ribbon on the flap. The ribbon, in accenting colors, is repeated on the body of the bag to continue the flow of the design. The machine stitching, in contrasting colors, provides an interesting detail for this conservative bag. The lining, of medium-weight fabric, is a colorful print, harmonizing with the colors of the ribbon. The size of the bag is 2′ × 3′.

A piece of rust suede is combined with crochet in this bag. A brass belt buckle, fastened with a strip of the same suede, is tied to the flap. Brass rings are sewn on the top edge of the purse, and a suede scrap becomes the handle. Holes are punched in this strap, and it is tied with a square knot.

Made by Jonda Friel. Photo by Francine Moskovitz.

Made by Francine Moskovitz.

Two large brown leather scraps in interesting shapes are made into a bag. They are fastened together with black jute crochet on the side panels. The edges are accented with black jute stitching.

The unicorns in medieval tapestries were the inspiration for this purse. A detailed weaving of this mystical animal is the focal point. The handles are hardwood, which is hand-carved and sanded. The design of the handles is created by two horns joined at the top. The leather is fastened to the wood with screws.

A brown leather scrap is appliquéd to the mustard suede body to make this handsome tote. Two large holes are cut through both layers on each side of the bag to accommodate the corded handles.

Made by Sioux Guerin.

74

This body bag has a shoulder strip and "belt" that fastens around the body. The front of this purse-snatcher's foil is a pin weaving of wool yarns and leather strips. The back and straps of the bag are light blue leather, with an extra woven piece on the flap for decoration. This fitted design offers freedom for shopping and other activities.

Two ties attached to the bag pass through two slits in the belt.

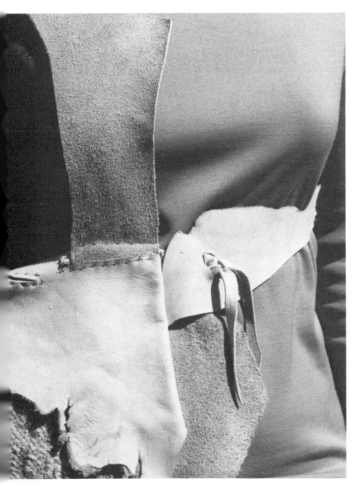

This contemporary chest piece is inspired by an authentic Indian breastplate. The leather pouch at the bottom is a container for special treasures. Strips of latigo leather provide the rigid framework. Holes are punched in these strips, to which wooden beads, buttons, and paper beads are threaded. The paper beads (the long white ones) are rolled and shellacked. The shoulder straps are finger-woven. Buttonhole stitch is used to finish the edge of the slit.

Modeled by Mike Ericson.

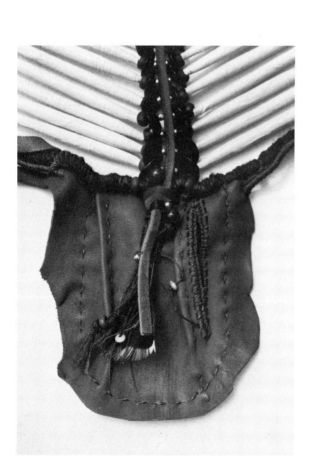

This "earth bag" is made of medium-weight leather, and it utilizes the folded-over raw edge of the leather as the focal point. The handle is thick (3/16") latigo leather, cut in the desired shape. The cut edges are dyed to match the handle. Many interesting shapes can be easily cut with a utility knife. The drawing shows several possible designs for purse tops/handles.

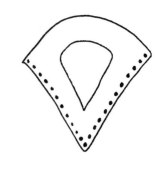

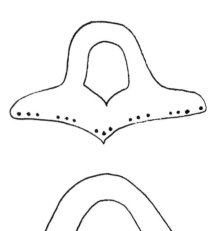

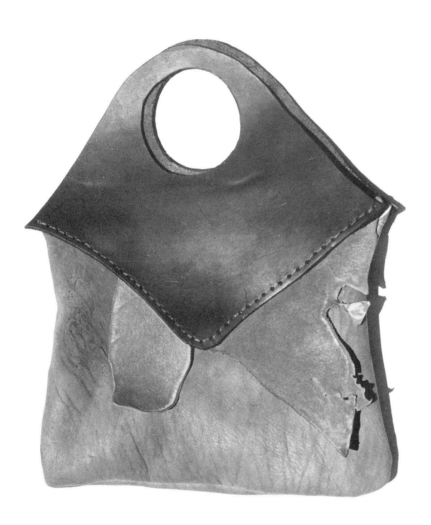

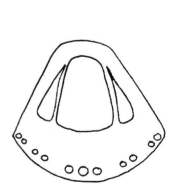

This neckpiece of soft leather was constructed on the same principle as an African basket container called a *kakongo.* The handle and side straps are laced in buttonhole stitch with waxed linen thread. The cover and the pocket are held together by a rolled leather strap that is long enough to go around the neck. The strap is sewn to the right-hand side of the pocket, and it extends through a hole in the cover and down through the other side, fastening to the left-hand side of the pocket. The opening is created by moving the top stick and the cover up, exposing the pocket inside. The sticks at the top and the bottom are optional handsome touches. The pattern for this pouch appears in chapter 7. Another example of this type of bag is shown in chapter 5.

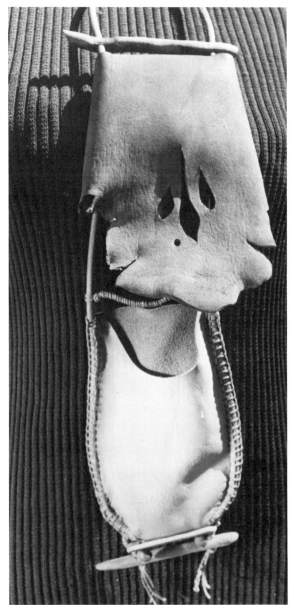

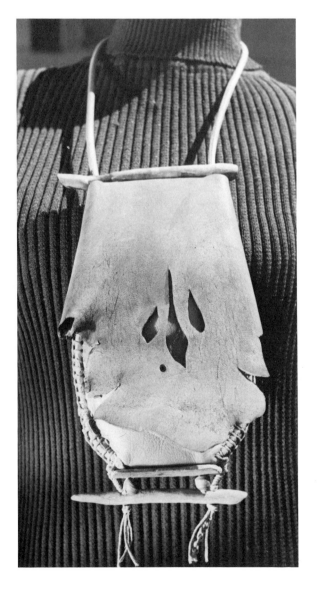

This beaded shoulder bag is made of dark brown and rust-colored leather. The double-headed bird design is sewn onto fabric and then appliquéd to the bag. Small pencil pockets on the sides are incorporated in the design of the handle. There are also pockets on the front and back.

This elegant belt pouch is trimmed with several shades of red beads, which are sewn directly onto the split sheepskin.

Made by Pat Smiley.

5
Basketry

There are a variety of ways and materials that can be used to make a basket. Whether you use yarns and commercially prepared materials or natural grasses and reeds, the techniques and the results are just as interesting.

COILING

Coiling is the easiest method of "sculpturing" a handbag or carryall. It is a fascinating technique, a little time-consuming but well worth the effort.

Equipment: a yarn needle, a pair of scissors, and a small pair of pliers are all you need.

Materials: the core is the foundation of the container. Which material to use for the core depends on the kind of bag you wish to make. Thin rope for clothesline can be used for an especially sturdy container. For a softer effect jute, chalk line, or upholstery welting can be utilized. One type of jute that is great to use is called "many-ends jute." It can be coiled and divided, then wrapped or coiled again. The size of the core also determines the weight of the container. If your bag is to be large, consider the overall weight in choosing your material. Almost any yarn can be sewn over the core. Good choices include wool, jute, raffia, or acrylics.

Method: the diagram shows the steps involved in coiling.

1. To start, wrap the core with the yarn for about 5" or the length of the first row. This length folded in half makes an oval shape; a shorter length makes a round shape.
2. To fasten the oval (or circle), fold the end over and continue wrapping over the two ends.
3. Work the stitch on the core, wrapping around it twice and sewing once into the previous row. The stitches should be pulled tightly to make a firm container.

Note: To add a new strand of yarn, hold the short strand together with the core. Add a new strand of yarn, holding all together. Continue sewing.

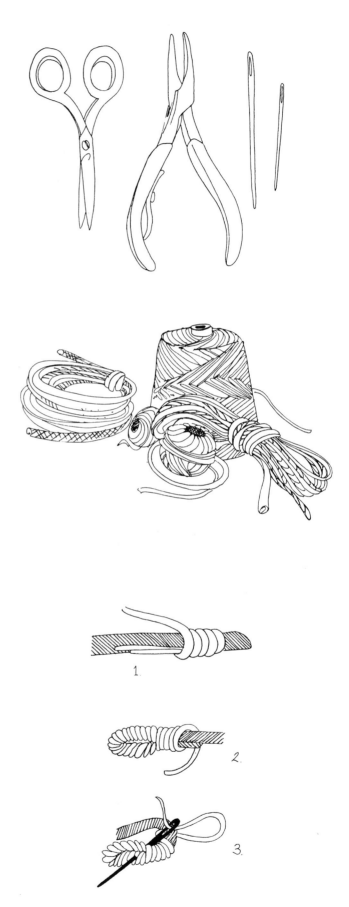

Basic stitches: the diagram shows some of the basic stitches of coiling.

1. The lazy-squaw stitch is probably the most common coiling technique. The pattern is achieved by repeating the following two steps: wrap over the core once, then wrap over the core and into the previous row.

2. The Peruvian coil weave is a variation of the lazy-squaw stitch. Simply wrap over the core three or four times, then wrap over the core and into the previous row and repeat.

3. The figure-eight stitch is, as its name implies, a stitch worked over two rows of the core simultaneously in a figure eight.

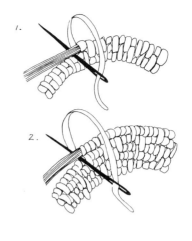

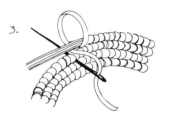

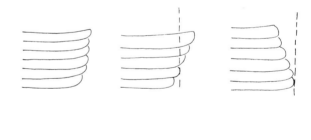

Shaping: to make the bottom of the basket, keep the coils flat. As you sew the stitches over the core, lay one row to the outside of the next row. When the bottom is the desired size, lay the core on top of the previous row and continue sewing. The shape of the vertical sides can be controlled by manipulating the core. Pulling tightly on the core will narrow the container. For a wider shape loosen the tension and lay the coil at the edge of the previous row.

Finishing: when the container is finished, cut the core on a long diagonal and continue sewing over it until it is covered completely. Insert the needle into the last few stitches and pull the thread through.

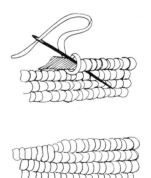

Surface decoration: surface areas can be built up with coiling and wrapping. Interesting items can be added to make the purse more individual, such as mirrors, beads, or other treasures. For ideas see chapter 6.

Handles: coat-hanger wire and a rope "core" make it possible to shape a handle of substance. First bend the wire to the desired shape, using a pair of pliers. Then hold a piece of ⅜" rope together with the wire and wrap the entire first row. Coil the second row in one of the stitches shown in this chapter.

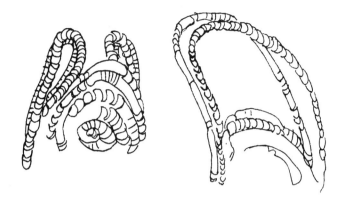

A handle can be made while the body of the purse is being coiled. At the appropriate place for the handle, stop coiling and wrap a piece of rope as long as the strap is to be. Coil the strap to the other side of the bag to attach. A handle can be added when the bag is finished by making the loops of wrapped rope part of the design.

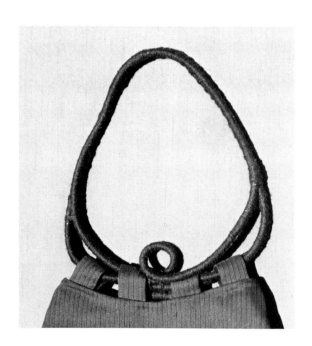

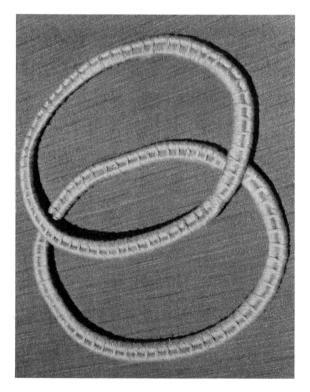

This photograph shows another example of wrapping and coiling over wire and ropes.

REED METHOD

Reed baskets are as old as time and yet as new as tomorrow. The techniques used then and now are basically the same.

Equipment: the tools needed for this type of basket making are minimal and easily accessible: a sharp knife, utility shears, a board for cutting on, and a pail or dishpan.

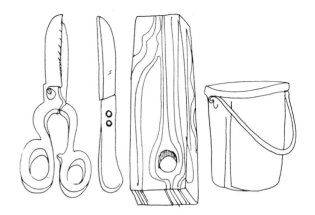

Materials: the choice of materials is very large, for, instead of gathering reeds from your immediate environment, you can purchase a variety of types and combine them with local plant life. Commercial materials include reeds, both round and flat; cane; sea grass; and raffia. Some natural materials to gather are corn husks, willow reeds, palm fronds, gladiola leaves, or other bladelike leaves and grasses. Dry the fibers, then soak them before using.

Method: to make a reed basket, you first have to prepare your materials. Soak the reeds in a freshwater river or lake—or an ample-sized pail or dishpan.

1. Cut stakes (or uprights) for your basket from fairly thick reeds (#5 or #6) two and one-half times the depth desired. For a small basket cut eight pieces 20″ long and one piece 10″ long. An odd number of stakes is needed.

2. Cut 1″ slits in the center of four of the reeds.

3. Slide the four uncut reeds through the four cut ones.

4. The reeds should be centered—equal lengths on both sides of the slit. Add the extra short reed between the two pairs as shown.

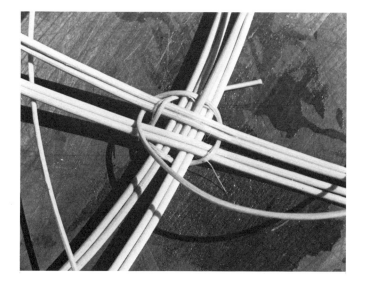

5. Start weaving one thin reed over and under two stakes at a time, treating the short one as a pair. Push the weaving reed as close to the center as possible. With a thicker reed this would be difficult to do. After weaving about three rows, separate the stakes into 17 individuals rather than pairs.

6. To start a new piece of reed, overlap the two reeds and continue on with a new piece. If the end of the previous piece shows or sticks out, cut it at an angle close to the stake.

7. After you have woven 4" or 5", you can start using thicker reeds.

8. If the reeds dry out, wet the entire basket: it is very important to keep them wet, or at least damp, so they won't split.

9. To shape the basket, the stakes can be tied together. Let them dry so they "remember" the shape. Then rewet when work is resumed.

10. Here is the finished product, a utility basket 15" high and 12" in diameter. The reed ends are cut at an angle. The tops of the stakes are soaked thoroughly, turned, and inserted in with the next stake.

DESIGN IDEAS

This method of transporting a heavy load has been universal since primitive times. The decorative band around the center is finger-woven. The ends are wrapped, and a few stoneware beads are attached.

Flat reeds ¼" wide are shaped over a coffee can to make this berry-picking basket. Round reeds are used for the weaving and the handle.

This is a basketry example of an African *kakongo.* Two plaited mats are folded and stitched together to make this bag. The wrapped handle slides through the holes on the cover. It is then fastened to the sides of the bottom half and left loose across the bottom, where feathers and beads become the focal point.

If a pot-luck supper is on the social calendar, a coiled casserole carrier would be a good project. The hot dish may be left in the carrier since it also serves as a hot pad.

This small purse is made in the coiling technique. Shades of fuchsia, maroon, and dusty rose wool are wrapped over a sisal rope core. Small mirrors are fastened behind the circles of the wrapping. The handle is wrapped and fastened through loops made on the sides of the bag.

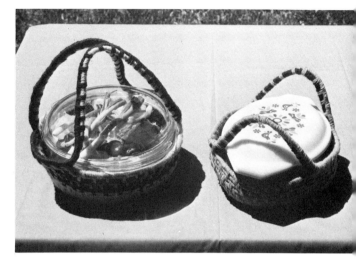

Made by Lilly Carlson.

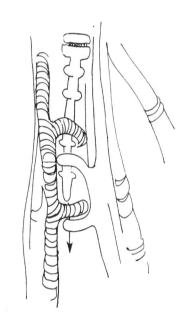

This large tote bag is truly a carryall. Coiling is done in a large circle, with colors gradually changing from yellow to orange, red, wine, and purple, so it looks like a brilliant sunset. The fastening device is a wood rod that slides through loops.

Shaped coiling and latigo leather are superbly combined in this purse.

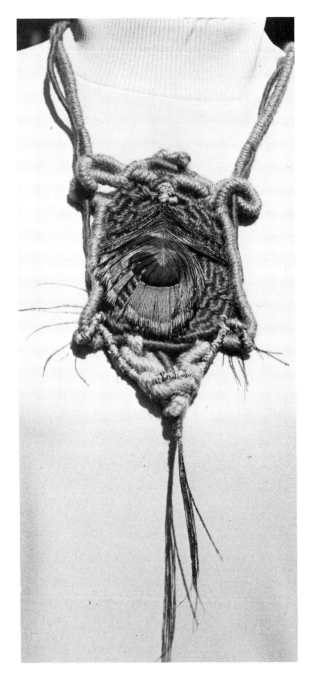

This neckpiece, which has a small pocket on the back, is coiled in shades of green, teal, and turquoise blue to correspond to the hues in the peacock-feather decoration.

Here the leather is punched and hand-stitched with linen. The fibers used for the coiling are jute, wool, and linen. The core is heavy jute and sisal. The leather is a mustard-gold color, which blends well with the natural and beige fibers.

This handsome basket, designed to carry Navajo spindles and fleece, is 32″ high. Yucca and aloe fibers are plaited together. This container reaffirms the concept that the functional can be beautiful.

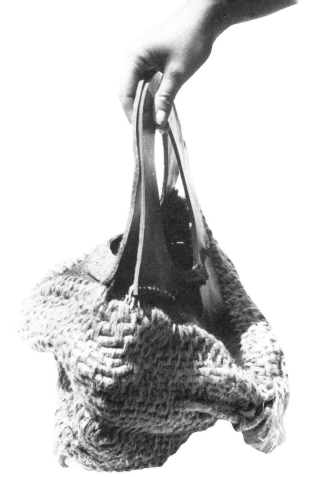

Made by Virginia Jeffries.

The handles of this basket are fashioned by wrapping yarn over a coat-hanger wire and knotted rope. They are then fastened to a shaped piece of cardboard. The warp of flat reed is attached to the handles and wrapped around the cardboard. The wefts are natural materials—dracaena, various grasses, and gladiola leaves. The muted colors and the pleasing form make this large bag (21″ × 28″) an outstanding example of basketry.

Indian inspiration is a very prominent factor in this contemporary cradle board. The frame is constructed of curved catalpa branches, which are dried and lashed together with heavy twine. Canvas webbing makes comfortable shoulder straps for the bearer. The "hood" is shaped with a network of flat reeds, which are inserted through holes drilled in the top side of the frame and joined in back. This network is then covered with cream-colored cotton-rag strips in a soumak stitch. The top of the "hood" is made of coiled cotton rags and sunny yellow and warm rusty-brown wool. The front pad is also coiled, using jute roving and grasses as the core. Canvas side panels are laced to keep the passenger secure.

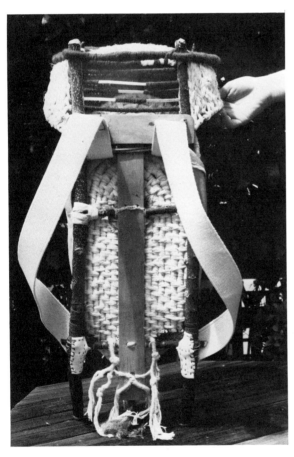

Made by Diane Ericson and modeled by Paula Giannini.

Natural yarns ranging in color from cream to dark brown make this coiled shoulder bag especially handsome. The core is clothesline, and the only decorations are three small bones, with feathers attached to the ends.

Made by Barbi Racich.

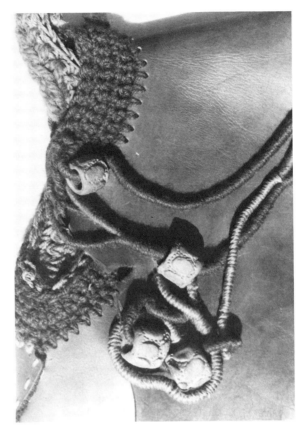

6
Supplementary Techniques

Basic techniques, of course, are very important, but the finishing touches really make a project distinctive. Surface treatments such as wrapping, yarn beads, or feathers and mirrors are the pièces de résistance.

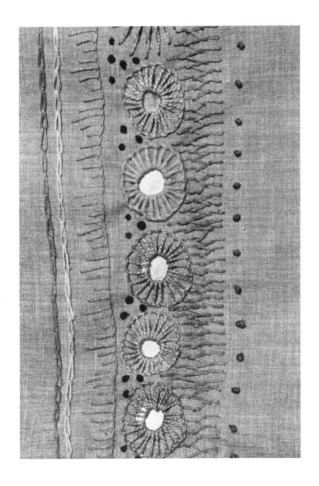

TASSELS

The diagram shows you how to make a beautiful tassel.

1. Wrap yarn around a piece of cardboard the length you want the tassel to be.
2. Insert an extra piece of yarn under one end and tie tightly. Cut the yarn at the opposite end.
3. To finish the tassel, wrap some yarn around the tassel about one-quarter of the distance from the tied end and fasten the thread. Embroider the band if desired. The decorative band can be made of scraps of lace, ribbon, fabric, or leather instead of yarn.
4. The top can also have a crocheted "slipcover."

YARN BEADS

Yarn beads are made by wrapping yarn around a strand to form balls and then embroidering them.

1. Warp yarn around strand.
2. Fasten the yarn to the strand.
3. Sew over the yarn ball with various threads of your choice.
4. Embellish the bead with embroidery stitches. Small beads and other treasures can be applied.
5 and 6. Finished beads.

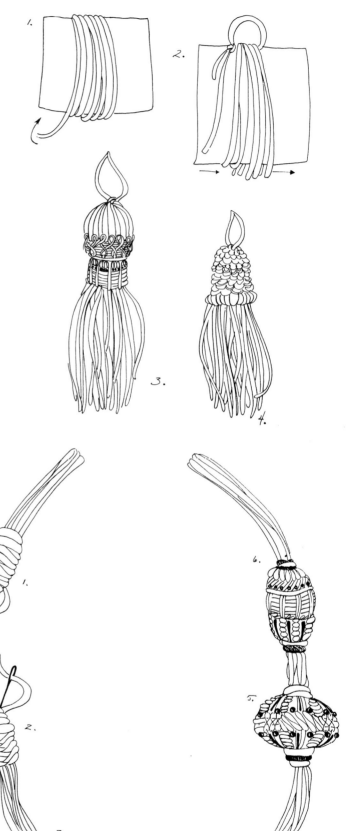

FEATHERS

This is an ancient Indian technique for applying feathers.

1. Start by making a lark's-head knot over the quill.
2. Bend the quill down towards the feather. Insert the needle and wrap over both needle and quill. Continue to wrap down towards the feather until the stem of the quill is covered.
3. Thread the needle with wrapping thread and pull it through to the end of the stem. At this point both threads are coming out at the same place.
4 and 5. By threading one of the wrapping threads through the loop made by the folded quill, the direction of the feather can be controlled.

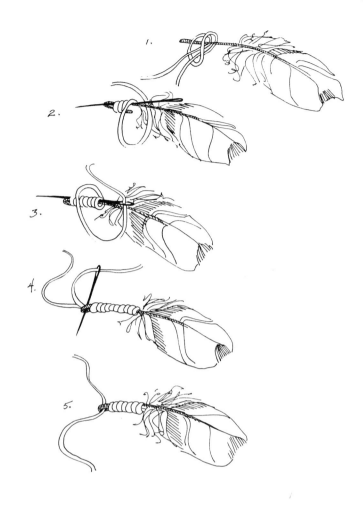

MIRRORS

The diagram explains how easy it is to insert mirrors in your work.

1. Take four stitches across the sides of the mirror, pulling *tightly* to hold fast.
2. Baste a line for a perfect circle if this is important. Make a buttonhole stitch by inserting the needle under the cross lines and taking up a small bit of fabric.
3. Continue stitching until the whole circle is filled in.

Note: shi-sha mirrors from India or Pakistan, available in bead shops, are made for cloth embroidery, but small commercial ones or even bits of mirrors work equally as well. The drawing shows one way to embroider mirrors into your work.

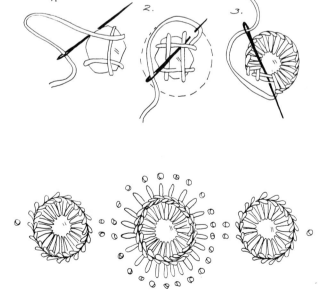

RIBBON

Ribbon is easy to use and readily available in a wide range of colors.
1. Mitering corners adds a professional touch. It can be accomplished by sewing a diagonal line.
2. Mitering can also be done by making an overhand knot.
3. Braiding ribbon, then appliquéing it onto fabric, adds a pleasing texture.

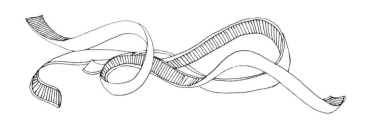

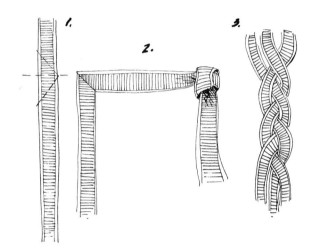

LEATHER BUTTONS

Buttons made of soft suede or smooth leather make attractive decorative accents as well as being useful.
1. Cut a long triangle.
2. Punch two small holes at the pointed end to sew through.
3. Roll the leather tightly from the wide end and mark with a pencil where the slits should be cut.
4. Insert the point through the slit and sew on.

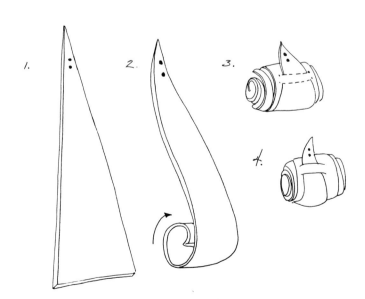

WRAPPING

This wrapping technique can be used over almost any material. In addition to yarn, you can wrap around leather strips, wire (to form into shapes), or groups of threads that are wrapped for a few inches, then regrouped and wrapped again. Wrapping with flexible wire can be very handsome.

1. Take a piece of yarn, double it, and pin the "folded" end to something sturdy to create tension. This is the base for your wrapping.
2. Take another piece of yarn, about 3' long. Use it double if it is thin. Place several inches of it parallel to the piece to be wrapped. Starting near the top, wrap the yarn around and around clockwise, covering the base.
3. To finish off the wrapping, simply insert a yarn needle pointing towards the beginning end. Thread wrapping yarn into the needle.

4 and 5. Pull the thread tight and cut off.

Note: If the wrapping thread becomes too short, hold the short end in with the thread being wrapped and start a new thread in the same way you started the first one.

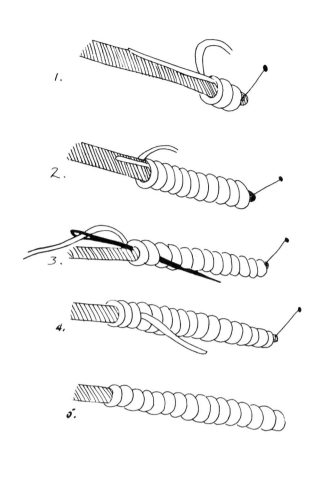

Wrapping can be used in many other ways. An especially interesting one is to combine it with soft fabrics such as silk, cotton, rayon, or velveteen, which can be stuffed with seed pods, beads, or marbles.

1. Put one bead on a small square of fabric. If you are cutting a large piece of fabric, figure out how much you will need for the wrapping.
2. Cover the "stuffing" with the fabric and wrap the yarn at the base to enclose the bead or pod.
3. Fasten the yarn with a needle.
4. A finished decoration.

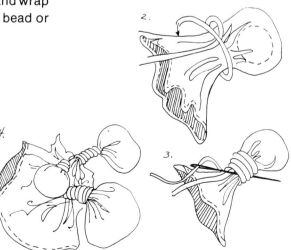

CORDING

Cord, string, or welting can be effectively stitched to make ridges.

1. Fold your fabric over the cord.
2. Pin the fabric close to the cord.
3. Stitch together by hand using one of the leather stitches described in chapter 4. Or stitch by machine, using a zipper foot to sew close to the cord.
4. For purse handles, especially, the cord can be inserted on two sides, with the raw edges turned in toward the center.
5. These ridges can be used in very decorative ways to make designs on fabric or leather.

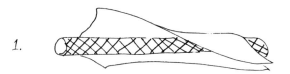

1.

2.

3.

4.

5.

WIRE CAGE

This cage makes an attractive ornament for holding treasures such as rocks or shells.

1. Leaving 1″ of wire at the top of the shell, bend the wire down on one side and make a loop at the bottom. Bend the wire up the other side to the top.
2. Wrap the wire around the top, making a quarter turn.
3. Bend the wire down the third side and wrap it around the loop one and one-half times.
4. Bring the wire up to the top on the last side and wrap the wire around a loop, made by bending the extra wire that was left at the beginning.

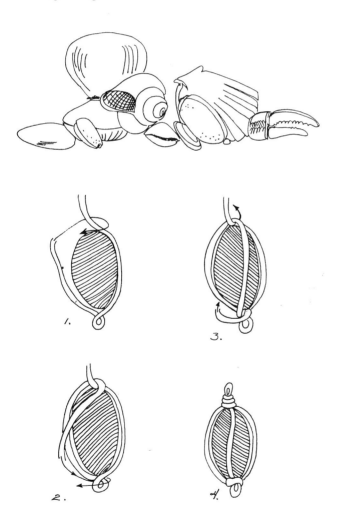

7
Pattern Ideas

Inspiration for a shaped container can come from many unusual sources, so be aware of various basic—or rare—forms that can be used to make a purse. A carryall can be as unique as your signature. Children as well as adults can make and enjoy using the containers shown in this book. Almost any of these designs can be made smaller for a child's purse or pack. Reducing the adult size by one-third is a good rule of thumb. Allowing a child to create his own design makes the container more meaningful. We hope the following pattern suggestions help you to design unique bags.

BASIC RECTANGULAR BAG

1. Pattern laid out.
2. The handle can extend down the side of the bag as a gusset.
3. The flap is a great place for ornaments and detail.

GATHERED HANDBAG

1. This is one side, so cut two sets. The center-piece can be any rigid material such as leather, wood, or fabric (underlined).
2. Gather fabric and adjust to fit the center. Stitch to the center.
3. Attach handles to the top of the bag. Put the pieces of fabric right sides together, stitch the sides and bottom, and turn inside out.

NEWSPAPER POUCH

1. The cutout becomes a pocket.
2. The handle can be rope, wood, or leather.
3. To make a roomier bag, a gusset (A) can be inserted on the side. Why not use a different material?

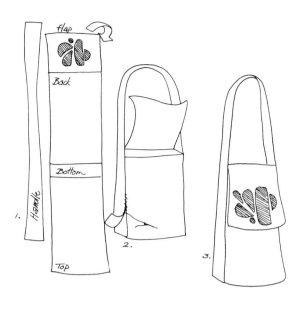

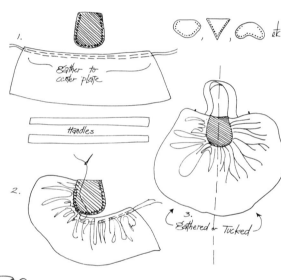

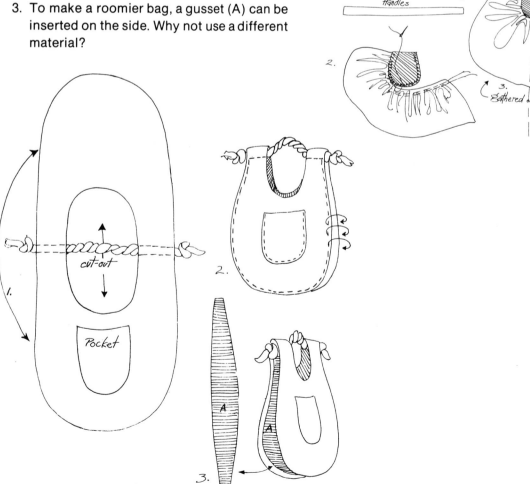

NECK POUCH

1. The lower half of the purse is on the left; the top half, on the right.
2. Handle. The top slides up and down on the leather cord, which is fastened to the lower half by stitching along the sides.
3. Finished purse, fastened, with the top partially covering the bottom.

SUNRISE BAG

1. Pattern opened flat, including handle.
2. Side gusset—make or cut out two of them.
3. Fold in the middle and sew the gussets to the sides.

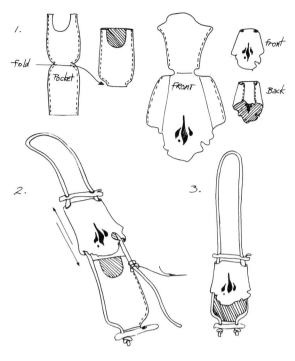

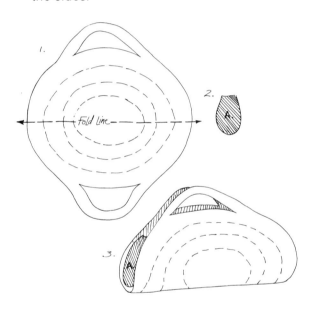

WHEELCHAIR BAG

This carryall can be clipped to the back of the wheelchair, or you could attach rings to each side to slide onto the handles.

1. Front and back, showing the fold line at the top, "pockets" for the clips to slide into (A and B), large bank clips or rings (C), and a piece to appliqué a decoration on the front (D).
2. Sew the "pockets" for the clips to the back. Appliqué and stitch the design.
3. Sew the side seams. Turn in the facing at the top and fasten.
4. Slide the bank clips into the pockets and fasten.

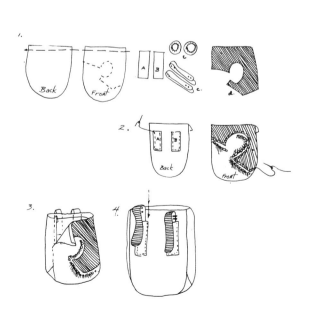

"PICTURE-FRAME" BAG

1. (A) is the front lining; (B), the front piece. Cut out the circle and face the opening in the front piece with bias tape. Cut out the fabric and lining for the back the same size as the front. Sew front piece and lining together, turn, and press flat. Sew back piece and lining together, leaving 3" or 4" so it can be turned to the right side.
2. Sew grosgrain ribbon to the handle and the gusset.
3. Stitch the front and back to gusset.
4. Baste the inset weaving, stitchery, or appliqué in place—this makes it easy to change with your mood.

ENVELOPE CLUTCH BAG

1. The corners are the flap, sides, and bottom. The dotted lines show where to fold.
2. Fold in the sides and bottom to form the front of the clutch and stitch together.
3. A snap can be used as a fastener.
4. The shape of the front flap can be decorated in any technique desired.

"MILK-CARTON" BAG

1. Cut the fabric double and use stiff interfacing. Stitch together and turn.
2. Fold on the lines as shown. Stitch the handles and turn.
3. Fasten the open side of the bag together. Attach the handles and fasten the bottom securely.
4. The points at the top can snap together or be left open.
5. Both ends can be sewn together, with a zipper at the opening.

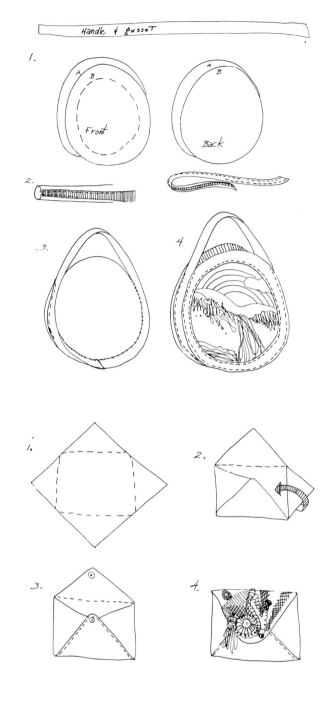

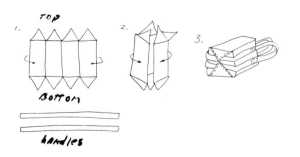

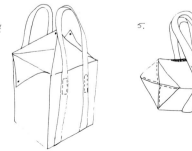

GATHERED SATCHEL

1. Tie the ends, cut to the desired length.
2. Gather the side gusset to fit the U-shaped curve of the purse center.
3. This gusset becomes part of the front and back of the satchel.

SADDLEBAG

1. Cut the back and front pockets of sturdy material or leather. The drawstring and the loops can be core, ribbon, or leather.
2. Sew the pockets to the back and turn to the right side. Attach the loops.
3. Attach drawstrings to the sides of the bag, thread through the loops and tie.

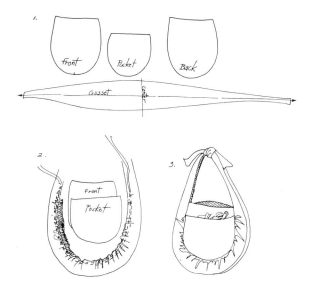

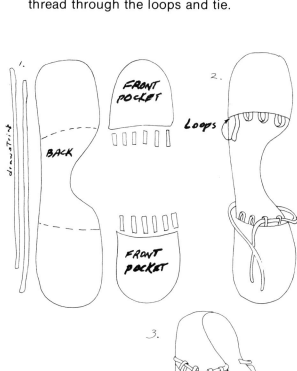

Bibliography

Beutlich, Tadek. *The Technique of Woven Tapestry.* Watson-Guptill, N.Y., 1967.

Birrell, Verla. *The Textile Arts.* Schocken Books, N.Y., 1973.

Christopher, F. J. *Basketry.* Dover, N.Y., 1952.

DeDillmont, Therese. *Encyclopedia of Needlework.* DMC Library, N.Y., Joan Toggitt Ltd.

D'Harcourt, Raoul. *Textiles of Ancient Peru and Their Techniques.* University of Washington Press, Seattle, 1962.

Hamlyn, Paul. *Tapestries from Egypt.* Hamlyn Ltd., reprint, Czechoslovakia, 1968.

Howard, Constance. *Inspiration for Embroidery.* Charles T. Branford, Newton Centre, Massachusetts, 1966.

Karasz, Mariska. *Adventures in Stitches.* Funk & Wagnalls, N.Y., 1959.

Keller, Ila. *Batik—The Art & Craft.* Charles E. Tuttle, Rutland, Vermont, 1971.

Krevitsky, Nik & Ericson, Lois. *Shaped Weaving.* Van Nostrand Reinhold, N.Y., 1974.

Laurel, Alicia Bay. *Living on the Earth.* Random House, N.Y., 1970.

Laury, Jean Ray. *Quilts and Coverlets.* Van Nostrand Reinhold, N.Y., 1970.

Mackenzie, Clinton D. *New Design in Crochet.* Van Nostrand Reinhold, N.Y., 1973.

Meilach, Dona Z. *A Modern Approach to Basketry.* Crown, N.Y., 1974.

Meilach, Dona Z. *Contemporary Leather.* Henry Regnery, Chicago, 1971.

Meilach, Dona Z. *Creating Art from Fibers and Fabrics.* Henry Regnery, Chicago, 1972.

Navajo School of Indian Basketry. *Indian Basket Weaving.* Dover, N.Y., 1971.

Plath, Iona. *The Decorative Arts of Sweden.* Dover, N.Y., 1966.

Robertson, Ronald G. *Contemporary Printmaking in Japan.* Crown, N.Y., 1965.

Index